The Game of Politics

American Government Simulations (2005-06)

Participant's Manual

Donald R. Jansiewicz

Preface

This non-traditional work has been written to help students in the American Government course and other venues to understand the political system from an insider's perspective, as well as from a human perspective. Participants will see legislative, executive and judicial decision-making take place on routine matters, and also see how our complex political environment places other issues on the public policy agenda. Although the characters and situations are fictional, the simulation is designed to describe real patterns within the American political process.

I have chosen to design simulations that put the emphasis on actual emotions and human drama. I have refrained from using an artificial scoring system. Winners in the macro and micro simulations will see their results, but more importantly, they will feel them. Conversely, those who do not get the most of what there is to get will feel a sense of loss. The net effect is to transform a classroom or conference into an experience that will have a long-term impact on the learner.

The macro and micro simulations are designed to achieve specific learning objectives and nurture interest in American politics. In this exercise, participants assume a variety of critical political roles at the national level of our system. Through these roles, they interact with each other and respond to pressures from the political environment. Out of all of this pulling and tugging, public policies emerge and conflicts are temporarily resolved.

The macro and micro versions of **The Game of Politics**© are set four to six years in the future, about one year after the election of a new President. Depending on the simulation that is used, proposed legislation might be considered along with a highly realistic budget. Supreme Court cases may also decided during the simulation.

This *Participant's Manual* contains three chapters and is supplemented by other materials (75 biographies, 180 bills, a budget and eight Supreme Court cases) that can be found in the appendices. These additional materials are designed to make the experience more realistic.

The Game of Politics© project progressed from idea to print over the course of several decades of teaching American government. Over the years, my students have been effective teachers and helped me work through a multitude of organizational details. Their efforts are deeply appreciated.

Finally, I want to dedicate this effort to my family, who make it all worthwhile.

Donald R. Jansiewicz
Baltimore, Maryland

Table of Contents

Chapter One

Serious Games: a Creative Way To Learn

This introductory chapter explores four closely related topics. First, It explains that games—especially simulations or serious games—are an extremely effective and useful way to promote learning. Then, it addresses the utility of games for the teaching of Political Science. Next, it demonstrates that **The Game of Politics**© macro and micro simulations are a very useful way to learn about our national political process. Finally, it suggests how you can become involved in this new learning experience.

Learning Through Games

Each of us has been learning all of our lives, both in and out of the classroom. Ironically, some of our most significant learning experiences are informal, and occur in non-threatening environments. We learn through free and open-ended discussions; we learn through trial and error; and we learn by imitating those whom we respect. In all of these significant learning events, the emphasis is on some sort of experience that allows for participation, exploration and creativity.

In this repertoire of informal activities, some of our most valuable learning experiences have occurred through innocent and not-so-innocent games. Our childhood experiences taught us something about what is expected of adults. We have learned about basic economic ideas by playing monopoly. We have learned traditional images of morality by playing "Star Wars." And, we have been learning about sex and sexual roles through an increasingly detailed game between males and females—as played by children, teenagers and adults.

We must understand that these game-like learning experiences do not necessarily produce absolute truth. In fact, some of our game experiences have distorted reality, as perhaps they were designed to do. Nevertheless, each of these games are real learning experiences in that they teach us something about life and how we are expected to live and act. In a sense, they are a dress rehearsal for reality. Games allow us to discover freely the rules and parameters of life. They produce significant increments in learning without the threat of insidious pop quizzes.

Given the fact that innocent games are such a powerful instrument for learning, it is reasonable to expect that we could design and participate in more serious games in an effort to learn more sophisticated material. A sophisticated, well-structured serious game allows us to approach complicated subject matter with the natural curiosity and creative urge that we all possess. Serious games allow us to seek out and perhaps discover the sophisticated principles of a complex world. Serious games encourage us to discover these principles by allowing us to find them on our own terms. We learn the principles by acting them out and reflecting on what we have done; we learn by doing. Instead of learning about complex theories in terms of vague abstractions, we are in a situation to discover these same theories and perhaps discover other things in the process.

Serious Games and the Study of Politics

The study of politics or collective decision-making is particularly open to the use of games. In fact, politics itself can be viewed as a serious game involving large numbers of players who cope with certain rules and use sophisticated strategies to pursue high stakes. It seems quite natural then to use a game to study a larger game. By viewing politics in terms of games, we are able to discover the principles of collective choice through our own authentic experience.

The use of games in the study of politics is not new. War games were used extensively by the Prussian military in the late 1860s. The German and Japanese military departments used sophisticated games for planning their strategies during the Second World War. Even today our own government uses games, especially in the area of national defense planning.

In addition to the use of political games by government, there are also a number of political games at all levels of education, ranging from elementary school through graduate programs. Many of these games focus on international politics, and there are games that focus on particular segments of our own government. At the end of this chapter, you will find a bibliography that illustrates how simulations or games have become a regular feature of the discipline of Political Science.

The Game of Politics Simulations

The Game of Politics© contains two types of simulation experiences. The macro simulation covers all three branches of the national government. The micro simulations each focus on a single slice of the political system.

The simulation that you are about to participate in will put you in one of the major roles in the American political system. You may be in Congress, the Presidency or the federal judicial system. You may even be placed in a media role. You will have routine duties to work on. Yet, more importantly, you will find yourself in the center of a highly charged and dynamic political environment where every issue competes with every other issue for attention. Throughout **The Game of Politics**© you and your colleagues will make decisions on normal public policy issues and will struggle with a variety of other domestic and foreign matters that will be thrown at you.

Getting Started

This simulation is designed to achieve five very broad learning objectives. At the end of the game, you should be able to:

1) identify formal and informal players who converge on various issues,
2) describe the material and symbolic stakes that motivate players,
3) assess the impact of rules on the decision making process,
4) note the strategies that are employed by various players, and
5) analyze the results of the political process.

Each of these objectives has a theoretical orientation that is inspired by the game framework. Participants will come to fully understand the theory through their own individual acts as political decision makers. That is, by pursuing your own goals within the context of a socioeconomic environment and decentralized political structure, you will be creating evidence that illustrates how the political system operates.

How to Proceed

In order to attain the objectives of the simulation, it is necessary for you to familiarize yourself with the most significant features of **The Game of Politics**©. Begin by acquainting yourself with the overall design of the simulation by reading Chapter 2 of this manual. This chapter will introduce each component and then pull all the pieces together.

Then, you should survey the roles or *Biographies* in Appendix A. Your simulation coordinator will provide you with a list of the roles that will be active during your simulation. You might want to note those roles that are most interesting to you as well as those roles that you would like to avoid. Your simulation coordinator may provide you with a form to indicate your preferences. This form will give you the opportunity to have an impact on your role assignment. The simulation coordinator would take this into consideration; however, there is no assurance that you will get your most desired roles.

At this point, you will be ready to turn to the public policy issues. If you are going to take part in one of the micro simulations, then, go directly to the appendix (B, C or D) that applies to you.

If you are going to participate in the macro simulation, begin with proposed *Legislation* provided in Appendix B. Note whether you are for or against this legislation as well as any amendments that would make the legislation more acceptable to you.

Then, if you are using the macro simulation, move on to the budget material. This manual provides you with past and proposed budget information. The budget is the lifeblood of our political system and it is of profound importance. Try to come up with your own figures and see how they compare to the budget results during the simulation. Make copies of the *National Budget* (Appendix C) so you can write with a pen on this material (or use a pencil).

Now, if you are using the macro simulation, turn to the Supreme Court *Cases* (Appendix D). Even though you probably won't be making decisions on these cases, ask yourself how you would decide them. It will be interesting to contrast your decisions with the decisions of your simulation's Supreme Court.

After surveying all of this material, you will be almost ready to participate in the macro or micro simulation experience. You will probably be assigned a role and should read chapter 3 of this Manual. That chapter will give you plenty of help in getting ready to enter into the political fray and make sense of your experience.

Rules of the Game

You will play by the same rules that actual participants use in our political system. The legislature will have complex rules for passing legislation and must, at times, overcome a veto by the President. The President will have wide discretion in making decisions, but can be stopped by an insistent Congress. The courts will have the capacity to limit the other two branches; yet the courts, in turn, can also be limited by the actions of legislators and executives. The First Amendment of the Constitution gives power to the media. However, the media may be constrained by the unwillingness of other players to cooperate with the press.

The rules of American politics will be a little confounding at first. Eventually, however, you will be comfortable in this new environment.

A fundamental rule of the simulation is to operate within the reality of the game. This means that **you should avoid solving your political problems by making up unrealistic things about yourself or others**. Use the resources that you have and work with these resources.

For Further Reading

Bennett, Paul W. "Teaching the Canadian Political Experience: A Simulation Game." History and Social Science Teacher 17.3 (1982): 131-38.

Brooker, Russell G. "Elections and Governmental Responsibility: Exploring a Normative Problem with Simulations." Simulation and Games 14.2 (1983): 139-54.

Brooker, Russell G. "Truth as a Variable: Teaching Political Strategy with Simulation Games." Simulation and Games 19.1 (1988): 43-58.

Deiner, John T. "Simulation Design: a Teaching Technique for Political Science." Social Studies 65:4 (1974): 157-60.

Foster, John L. and others. "Verstehen, Cognition and the Impact of Political Simulations: It is Not as Simple as it Seems." Simulation and Games 11.2 (1980): 223-41.

Fuller, Jack W. "Simulation in a Political Science Classroom." Improving College and University Teaching 21.4 (1973): 284-5.

Gilboa, Eytan. "Studying Mass Media Roles: The Use of Simulation in National and International Politics." Teaching Political Science 7.1 (1979): 73-88.

Kaarbo, Juliet and Jeffrey S. Lantis "Coalition Theory in Praxis: a Comparative Politics Simulation of the Cabinet Formation Process." PS: Political Science and Politics 30.3 (1997): 501-6.

Laver, Michael. Playing Politics: Games to Bring Out the Politician in Everyone New York: Oxford UP, 1997.

Nichols, Thomas, W. "Political Simulation for the Classroom." Social Studies Journal 9 (1980): 33-43.

Ray, Bruce. "A Legislative Simulation." Teaching Political Science 8.2 (1981): 213-16.

Vogel, Rex. "The Effect of a Simulation Game on the Attitudes of Political Efficacy." Simulation and Games 4:1 (1973): 71-79.

Walcott, Charles and Anne Walcott. Simple Simulations: A Guide to the Design and Use of Simulation/Games in Teaching Political Science. Washington D.C.: American Political Science Association, 1976.

Chapter Two

The Game of Politics

This chapter explains how **The Game of Politics**© is organized as well as how it operates. The chapter has been divided into four different sections that describe (1) the players, (2) the routine policy issues, (3) various Story Lines that your instructor will drop into the simulation and (4) how all the pieces fit together.

The Cast of Characters

All of the individual roles are described in the *Biographies* or roles (Appendix A). These biographies are presented in alphabetical order and give a brief background for the character as well as such things as party affiliation, committee memberships or leadership positions.

In all, there are 75 roles described in these biographies. It is more than likely that some of these roles will not be used in your particular simulation. Your simulation coordinator will provide you with a list of those roles that will be active, and you should highlight or check those roles (in Appendix A) that are part of your simulation. Skim through those particular roles. Get a sense of who is potentially in the simulation, as well as what these roles bring to the game.

There are four types of players within the macro and micro simulations. They are (1) legislative players, (2) executive players, (3) judicial players and (4) media players. The exact roles that will be used will depend on whether you are participating in the macro simulation or one of the micro simulations. Read *all of the following if you are using the macro* simulation. If you are in a *micro simulation*, read the following material that *applies to the micro simulation you are using*.

The **legislative players** in the macro and micro simulations are divided into the two houses of Congress and serve on various committees that scrutinize the legislative proposals. The Republicans have a majority in the House and on each House committee, and the Democrats have a majority in the Senate and its committees.

For the purpose of simplicity, each house has the same structure of STANDING COMMITTEES and these committees will concentrate on certain types of legislation. Consequently, you will find that individual Representatives and Senators are assigned to (1) the Internal Matters Committee, (2) the External Matters Committee or (3) the Government Operations Committee. These committees consider the bills that are part of this simulation and have the power to pass, amend or kill these legislative proposals.

If your simulation is large enough, each of the committees will be divided into subcommittees. These subcommittees consider and act on legislation prior to consideration by the committees.

Those bills that get through the committees are then sent on to the full House and Senate for consideration and reconsideration. If passed, the bill then goes to the

President for acceptance or veto. A two-thirds majority in each chamber can override a Presidential veto. Of course, legislators can always introduce new bills into the process.

The House has another type of committee, the RULES COMMITTEE, which reviews legislation after it gets through a House standing committee and before it goes to the full House for consideration. The Rules Committee acts as a traffic cop, scheduling when the bill will be heard, how much time will be allowed for discussion and what kinds of amendments, if any, can be considered.

The Senate does not have a Rules Committee. However, individual Senators have the power to place a hold on a bill and delay its consideration for a session. Senators also have the right to filibuster, or talk a bill to death.

In addition, each house also has a BUDGET COMMITTEE that considers the President's budget requests and recommends a budget to their respective chambers. This budget is then debated and amended in each house until a budget resolution is passed. This resolution sets up budgetary goals that can be altered by appropriations bills (later in the process).

It is often necessary for CONFERENCE COMMITTEES to be created to resolve differences between the House and Senate versions of the proposed legislation or the budget. The membership of an individual conference committee is chosen by the leadership in each house, and roughly reflects the balance of party control in each house. Generally, each conference committee contains three members from the House and three members from the Senate.

Because of the number of players within the legislative branch of government, it is necessary to have a rather structured pattern of leadership, as follows:

The Speaker of the House, Representative Villary, a Republican, maintains an orderly flow of work for the House and gives direction to the chamber. There are also leaders and assistant leaders for each party within the House and these leaders try to keep their parties together, particularly on key votes.

In the Senate, the day-to-day leadership is in the hands of Senator Meyers, a Democrat and the Majority Leader. Meyers also keeps order in the Senate and keeps legislation moving along. In addition to the Majority Leader there is a Minority Leader, plus assistant majority and minority leaders.

In situations in which a tie vote is expected, Vice President Rourke will probably preside over the Senate. The Vice President will be able to vote in those situations and will be able to break the tie.

There is also a leadership pattern within each of the committees in the House and Senate. Each committee has a Chair from the majority party as well as First and Second Vice Chairs who would temporarily take control in the absence of the committee chair. Even the minority party on each committee has a ranking member who will become the committee Chair in the event that the minority party becomes the majority party after the next election.

Those of you who are placed in a legislative role will gain new insight and appreciation for the Congress of the United States. You will find that the process is extremely complicated, and that legislation seems to crawl through the legislative obstacle course. It takes a major effort to quickly move legislation through the whole Congress.

There are also **executive players** within the macro and micro simulations. These players are (1) the President, (2) the Vice President and (3) members of the President's White House Staff.

Approximately one year ago, President Millworth was elected to the White House and that first year in office was a very difficult experience. The President had a relatively easy time getting legislative and budgetary proposals through the Senate. However, the President had great difficulty in gaining support from the Republican-dominated House. The President's marriage also dissolved shortly after taking office.

Within the simulation, the President will have to make recommendations on the legislation that is before the Congress and will have to submit a budget to the House and Senate. In addition, the President will have to cope with a number of domestic and foreign policy problems as well as a host of other issues.

One of the most important things for the President to do is to make effective use of his or her staff. The Vice President and the President's Advisors can be assets for a President who can't be in several locations at the same time.

Those of you who are selected to be part of the executive branch will come to understand the paradox of executive leadership. On one hand, the executive branch seems to be the dominant branch of government and the center of action. Yet, on the other hand, it does not have sufficient power to control events. It has to contend with a powerful Congress, other governments and a multitude of uncooperative individuals and groups.

The simulations may also have one or more **judicial players**. These players are purposefully kept apart from the rest of the normal legislative and executive activities. However, they are always "out there" and ready to make judicial decisions that will have just as much of an impact as Presidential and Congressional decisions.

Within the simulations, there are eight cases before the Supreme Court. These cases can be found in the appendices to this manual. The actual Supreme Court decisions will be announced later.

In addition, issues regarding interpretation of laws and procedures as well as Constitutional issues may arise within the context of the macro simulation. Decisions on these matters will have to go to one of the lower courts and may also go on to the Supreme Court. Such decisions will be made and announced as necessary.

If you are placed in a judicial role, you should take this responsibility seriously and not discuss the issues with legislative or executive players. Try to base your decisions on current legal precedents as well as your own understanding of the Constitution. When you have made your decision, it needs to be written out as a Supreme Court Opinion and given to the media for general announcement.

There are also one or more **media players** within the macro and micro simulations. These players work for major media companies, and these reporters have national reputations. The media will, in effect, describe what is taking place within the simulation.

The media will receive information from the simulation coordinator on a variety of news stories. Also, the media will obtain information from the many press conferences that take place during the simulation. In addition, the media will interview other players as well as outside participants. Then, the media summarizes this information and reports it at the beginning of each simulation session.

If you are selected for a media role, you will be under a unique set of pressures. There will probably be more information than you can possibly report on; consequently you will have to make choices. Even deciding which story will be the top story is an important judgment. Also, you will find that other players have mixed feelings about you. Some will want to contact you in order to publicize their points of view, while others will avoid you in order to minimize negative publicity. One of the toughest things for the media to do is to separate honest reporting of the facts from editorial opinion.

The Policy Agenda

In **The Game of Politics**© there are four kinds of routine types of policies that can emerge from either the macro or micro simulations. These policies are (1) legislation, (2) the budget, (3) executive orders, and (4) court decisions. Each these four types of policies involves different decision-making routines, and all have a different appearance.

These policies do not just drop out of the sky. Rather, they are the hard work of players who sort through the possibilities and make a collective commitment that is binding on American society.

In the macro simulation and some micro simulations (legislative, presidential), 180 different bills or **legislative proposals** compete for the attention of decision makers; individual legislators can also introduce additional bills into the process. Not all of the bills in the simulation, however, will be voted on, and only a few will actually be passed in one form or another by both houses of Congress and then receive the signature of the President.

There is also a trillion-plus dollar **national government budget** in the macro simulation and the micro budgetary simulation. You can examine historical material for the budget to help you gain some perspective on revenue and expenditure patterns. You will also find budget proposal information to help make your own budget.

The budget is automatically near the top of the agenda in American politics because our government can't continue without money. The President will make specific recommendations in terms of revenues and expenditures, as well as the deficit. These recommendations will then go through the Congressional budget committees, votes in each chamber, a conference committee and back to each chamber. The President cannot veto this budget resolution or plan. However, specific appropriations bills must be passed eventually, and these bills could be vetoed by the President (which would take a two-thirds vote of each house to override). There are many struggles that will take place over the budget. Ideas will rise and fall, and on occasion, odd things will get attached to the budget.

It is rare that everyone will be happy with the results at the end of the budget process. Most of the time, the budget players are just glad that some agreement was reached.

Within the macro simulation and one micro simulation, situations will arise in which the President will issue **executive orders**. These orders are specific responses to issues that are brought to the President, and they are based on authority that has been granted to the President by a past Congress. It is quite normal for the President to issue orders as long as these orders do not violate legislative intent. Executive orders will usually not receive the same type of attention as other types of policies. You will notice that there isn't even an appendix for executive orders in this manual. Yet, this murky status does not deny the fact that orders are policies, and they do make a difference in distributing advantages and disadvantages.

As the macro simulation and the Supreme Court micro begin, there are already judicial issues on the national public policy agenda. These issues are the **Supreme Court Cases** that are provided. Normally, you will just have to wait to see what happens to these cases, and your interactions with the judicial system will probably be minimal.

However, you may find yourself in some dispute in the macro simulation that can't really be decided within or between the legislative and executive branches of government. In that situation, you may become a party to a legal action, and you will be involved in a new case in the court system. In such a situation, your case will be heard by one of the lower federal or state courts, and you do have the right to appeal. But be forewarned that the Supreme Court controls its own agenda, and it may not even want to consider your case. In those situations, the decision of the lower court is binding.

Story Lines

One of the most unique things that you may discover about **The Game of Politics**© macro and micro simulations is how an alternate reality seems to take over and how you get caught up in the drama. Events will unfold that are beyond the bills, budget or court cases. These situations are varied in content and serve as a counterpoint to the normal activities of governing.

Within the simulations, you may encounter a variety of Story Lines that will evolve over the course of the game and will all be taking place simultaneously. Story Lines represent external forces that affect the political process.

Some of these stories revolve around proposed **legislation** in the simulations, as well as the **budget**. You will feel comfortable with these issues because they relate to the routine duties of government.

Yet, most of these Story Lines involve other matters that you will find to be both interesting and distracting at the same time. Some of these stories are the types of drama that also compete for your attention in the real world.

The simulation includes **domestic** Story Lines that center on struggles to get other items on the public policy agenda. Typically, these issues involve economic or social issues, and are quite intense. In addition, there will be Story Lines involving **foreign and military** policy. These issues will involve America's relationships with other nations in the world, which can sometimes flare up to a danger point.

In addition, you may confront other types of Story Lines within the macro and micro simulations. Some of you may find yourself involved with **constituency service** issues, and will be trying to promote the interests of those who elected you to office. Others of you will confront **wildcard** Story Lines, finding yourselves in very complex situations that may require difficult personal choices. To make things more complex, a limited number of **distractions** are included among the Story Lines.

In an overall sense, these Story Lines will round out your understanding of American politics. Through the Story Lines you will see that there is a whole lot more to American politics than just churning out legislation, budgets, executive orders and court decisions. You will see that governing involves a constant balancing act over a multitude of matters, some of which are trivial and some of which are issues of life and death. Without experiencing these "other" factors your understanding of American politics would be incomplete.

Putting It All Together

Each session of the macro and micro simulations will bring all of these pieces together. A typical session will begin with a report from the media that will summarize governmental decision-making activities as well as other events from the past simulation session. That news report will be followed by press conferences from participants in the simulation as well as other individuals or groups that are trying to gain support for their points of view. These news conferences, then, will be followed by legislative, executive and judicial activities in the macro simulation or selected policy activities in the micro simulation. And, any of these activities may be interrupted by more press conferences, or by other information that is coming in from various Story Lines.

Within the simulation, you will be pulled in two different directions. On one hand, you will be trying to do a good job with your assigned role. On the other hand, you will have to come to grips with other factors that keep you from doing your job. It is sometimes frustrating and confusing. Yet, it is always an important part of **The Game of Politics**©.

Chapter Three

Making The Most of This Experience

This last chapter of the manual is designed to explore the problems and opportunities that you will encounter as a participant in **The Game of Politics**©. It is divided into four basic areas of concern. They are as follows 1) assistance in adapting to a new, and undoubtedly different, way of behaving, (2) suggestions on how to design political strategies, (3) a review of strategic alternatives, and (4) a discussion of the relationship between the simulation and the five learning objectives.

Your New Role

At this point you might have feelings of quiet desperation. You may well fear that you really don't understand your role or that you don't know what to do first. From your initial reading of the materials, you may imagine that the game is stacked against you—that you are finished before you start.

It might comfort you to know that every participant in **The Game of Politics**© macro and micro simulations starts off feeling a little lost. Each and every player has the feeling that he or she cannot possibly come out ahead. Yet participants do get their feet wet in short order, and find that they can succeed at some of their goals in the game.

In designing the simulations, great care has been taken to ensure that *no one player has the upper hand*. Each role is constructed so as to give every player a relatively equal share of advantages and disadvantages. Those players who become "winners" do not do so because of a natural advantage. Rather, the "winners" are those who learn to overcome obstacles, develop creative strategies, and build a winning coalition.

Read your role biography carefully and note that it gives you a sense of personal history and gives you an identity within the big picture. However, it does not lock you into some form of behavior that is impossible for you to "act out." It would be most helpful if you viewed your biography as an anchor that gives you a sense of position within the simulation. However, these anchors should not be seen as being too restrictive. In reality, the biographies are your starting points and they give you a great deal of freedom to interpret, navigate and explore within reasonable limits.

Even with the freedom inherent in your role, you can still seek guidance from your simulation coordinator. Feel free to ask the coordinator how you might handle a particular situation or how you might carry out your role.

In all roles, it is necessary that you adapt your role to fit your own personality. Yet, it is also essential to adapt yourself to the demands of your new role. This process of blending yourself into a new role may be a little difficult at first. But as time passes, you will feel more and more comfortable. Your new role will eventually become more natural and familiar.

Your simulation coordinator may ask you to construct an analysis of your role. If so, this exercise will get you to understand your role in terms of goals, priorities, relationships with others, as well as strengths and weaknesses. This information can help you immensely, and will enable you to adapt to your role in a very short time.

Constructing Political Strategies

The importance of sound strategy cannot be overemphasized. Unless you carefully design workable plans of action, it is highly unlikely that you will be able to make any appreciable gains or even preserve the advantages that you already have. An individual strategy is the vehicle that will help you achieve your goals. Construct your strategies carefully and you will be gratified by the results.

Viable political strategies are designed on the basis of three very different foundations. These foundations or touchstones are:

1) your own interests,
2) your relationship to others, and
3) your sources of power.

Let us explore each of these foundations and come to understand why you must keep them in mind when designing your game plan.

Any successful strategy must be based first of all *on your own interests and goals* (see your biography). That is why it is imperative that you have a thorough knowledge of your goals and priorities. If you have completed a *Role Analysis*, you will see that you have already grappled with this issue. In reviewing your goals and priorities, you should begin to make some realistic judgments as to what you wish to accomplish. If you overestimate and try to achieve too much, you will probably accomplish nothing. On the other hand, if you underestimate and try to accomplish too little, the other participants will probably assume that you are willing to settle for less. Consequently, they may walk all over you.

Try to strike a balance. Perhaps you might benefit by selecting a maximum and minimum level of achievement. Or perhaps you can strike a balance by developing three or four packages of goals. In any case, give yourself flexibility so that you can be both aggressive and open to revision.

A second thing to look for in framing your strategy or strategies is to *be aware of your relationship to others*. It is inconceivable that you will be able to achieve your goals by acting unilaterally. Instead, it is advisable and generally quite necessary to develop coalitions with others. If you completed a *Role Analysis*, you will have a sound conception of those you can rely on for assistance. Your "allies" will be a good starting point in the development of a coalition. Quite often, however, it is necessary to go beyond your allies to develop enough political strength. You may find that it is necessary to take the in-between or neutral roles into consideration.

The third aspect of any viable political strategy entails a wise use of *your sources of power*. Your power can include such varied things as membership on a committee, the ability to vote, control of information, the capacity to veto as well as a multitude of other power sources. As you can imagine, an infinite amount of resources would undoubtedly allow any political actor to achieve all of his or her goals. In the real world, though, any player's resources are limited. If you did a *Role Analysis*, you will see that you do not have a surplus of political resources. Rather, you will note that your sources of strength are in short supply. Both on paper and in the actual game situation, you will see that your resources alone will not guarantee success.

Faced with the problem of scarce resources, you are going to have to decide how, when and for what purposes to use your power. You dare not spend all of your resources too fast for fear that you will be left powerless and vulnerable. Nor should you be too conservative, because unspent resources are of little value. It is in your best interest to strike a balance; spend your resources fast enough to attain your goals, but not so fast as to go broke in the process.

If you keep each of these foundations in mind, you should be able to devise strategies that are both creative and effective. By reminding yourself of your interests, your relations and your sources of power, you will certainly be in a position to adopt those strategies that are best suited to your needs and capabilities.

On another note, you should take the situation that you have in the simulation and work within the parameters of the simulation. DO NOT FABRICATE INFORMATION ABOUT YOURSELF OR OTHERS UNLESS YOU ARE PREPARED FOR NEGATIVE CONSEQUENCES FROM OTHERS.

Alternative Strategies

Those who play **The Game of Politics**© seem consistently to select strategies that are remarkably similar to the techniques used in the real world. The past has demonstrated that these strategies are both realistic and effective. Let us explore each of these alternatives so that you might make effective use of any or all of the techniques. These alternative strategies can be simply listed as follows:

1. appealing to the public;

2. persuading others;

3. manipulating the rules and structure;

4. determining who gets public office;

5. shifting responsibility;

6. bargaining with others through

      a. unilateral action,
      b. anticipated reaction,
      c. logrolling,
      d. logrolling over time,
      e. awarding sidepayments, and
      f. compromising;

7. depriving others; and

8. instilling myths and impressions.

1. Appealing to the public

One strategy that might be considered is the *public appeal*. By going over the heads of other participants, you can stir up public opinion and thus increase your supply of resources. Participants in the political process often use this strategy because it is quite economical. It does not cost you much in the way of resources and it is quite effective if used correctly.

You can use this strategy within the simulation by requesting to have a press conference. If handled properly, you can utilize the press conference to maximum advantage; you can increase your visibility, get the jump on adversaries or defend your position on the issues. The press conference allows you to reach the public directly without any intermediary.

A more subtle approach to a public appeal is to take your case to the media. If the media presents you or your views in sympathetic terms, then, the media will allow you reach the public indirectly and you won't have to respond to the questions that occur in a press conference.

In either approach to appealing to the public—press conference or going to the media—there is always the risk that you will get lost in the shuffle. Your particular message may be relegated to an unimportant status. If you are too excessive in your pursuit of public relations, you may alienate decision makers who will see you as a person who ignores their interests. Don't overuse publicity. It might backfire and prevent you from obtaining your goals.

2. Persuading others

The second strategy that you might wish to utilize is persuasion. Persuasion means using logical arguments about what is in the best interest of the public. Each of us uses this technique every day when we try to convince others to go along with us and accept our views. You can adapt this same strategy to your behavior in the game and use it to attain your personal goals.

One way of effectively using the strategy of persuasion is to combine it with a public appeal. A carefully worded statement to the press or a well-planned press conference can be effective if it emphasizes the "public interest" and appears to be logical.

You can also use persuasion by speaking privately with a decision maker or sending that decision maker a note. Again, in doing so, it is wise to emphasize what is good for everyone. However, you should not attempt to lay down a barrage of persuasive arguments. Such overkill could hurt you more than help you.

In addition to using persuasion though public appeals and personal contact with other decision makers, you might wish to use the persuasion technique in one of the committee meetings or on the floor of the House or Senate, or even in the judiciary and Administration. These meetings can provide you with a forum to make your case. Many participants in the game have routinely used such arenas to present logical arguments for or against a particular legislative, budgetary or legal matter, or other policy issue.

Although the persuasion strategy has much merit, it is limited in its utility. Political decisions are rarely decided on logical arguments alone. Decision makers would like to do "what is best for the public," but the decision-making process usually emphasizes attainment of private goals.

In order to use persuasion most effectively, you should use it often on the surface and supplement with more privately oriented strategies. The ideal situation is to be able to address yourself to a public interest that coincides with your interest and the interest of other political actors.

3. Manipulating the rules and structures

Another workable strategy is to manipulate the rules and structure of the game in order to favor your interests. This manipulation takes place because political decision makers realize that rules and structural arrangements benefit some more than others.

In manipulating the rules and structure, you must be aware of how various combinations of rules and structure will affect your goals. If you misperceive the impact, you may regret the expenditure of your resources. Be quite sure before you act. Don't fight for a change, or to maintain some rule or structural arrangement, unless you fully understand the consequences in terms of your interests. Consult with your simulation coordinator if you are uncertain about the impact of current rules and structures on your goals.

You should also be aware that this strategy of manipulation is very costly. In essence, you are spending precious resources for something that only indirectly affects you. This expenditure can be worthwhile, but you should not use this strategy alone. Remember that your resources are scarce, and all expenditures of resources should be carefully evaluated.

4. Determining who gets public office

An additional strategy or way of achieving your goals is to determine who gets public office. If you can assist another player in being elected or appointed to a particular position within the simulation, then that person may well be indebted to you. You can collect on that debt by asking the other player to use his or her new powers to help achieve your goal(s).

If you decide to use this strategy, you should be careful not to ask for too much. Remember that the other player has his or her own goals. Ideally you should be able to help someone who already agrees with you on the particular goals in question. Since such agreement is rare, you will probably have to limit what you expect of this other participant. Moreover, you should avoid giving that player the impression that you are only interested in your future. Nobody wishes to be viewed as just a pawn of someone else's personal interest.

Determining who gains office can be a highly beneficial political strategy. But it also has costs. If you use this strategy, you will have to spend a large portion of your resources and you must be sure that the expenditure will be worthwhile. It would be most unfortunate to expend resources and not realize a return. Before engaging in this strategy, take care to be sure that the recipient of your favor will not suddenly develop too much independence.

5. Shifting responsibility

One more political strategy that you might wish to employ is shifting responsibility. In this fifth strategy, you either take action or refuse to take action as determined by your interest. You can get the jump on the opposition, and define the problem in such a way that the solution conforms to your goals, by simply taking action and claiming that the responsibility is yours. You can also employ this strategy by refusing to take action. In doing this, you can escape a resource expenditure by throwing the problem into someone else's lap. This is especially useful if action would mean that you might have to act against your own interest.

This strategy can be extremely effective because it allows you to impose your own priorities on the situation. You can choose to usurp the decision-making power on those issues that interest you, and ignore potential action when it comes to matters that do not interest you or might hurt you.

The advantages of this strategy are quite obvious. The disadvantages are a little more difficult to detect. For example, it is harmful to engage in a power struggle over who has responsibility for an issue. Moreover, it can be disadvantageous to appear too aggressive in claiming responsibility or seem "wishy-washy" in constantly avoiding decision-making. If you can overcome these disadvantages, the art of shifting responsibility can net you payoffs in terms of your policy goals as well as a positive public image.

6. Bargaining with others

An extremely effective approach to political gain is the sixth strategy—bargaining. This approach requires that you invest some of your resources to aid another player in attaining his or her goal(s). In return for this outlay, you can possibly gain some of the other player's resources to help attain your own goals. In effect, this strategy of bargaining is premised on long-term mutual gain. Several varieties of the bargaining strategy follow.

Unilateral action

This variant of the bargaining strategy is simply to make decisions and take actions under the assumption that an unknown someone will benefit and may help you at a later point. The gains coming from this unilateral approach can be high, but it is still risky because the unknown person may not feel obliged to help you since he or she recognizes that the gains were purely accidental. That is, the recipient or gainer may perceive that you did not intend to help him or her in particular. Consequently, the recipient or "free rider" may not feel that he or she owes you a favor for your actions and instead believes that you only acted in your own interest.

Anticipated reaction

Another variant of bargaining is to anticipate who will be helped by your resource expenditure. By doing this and planning your actions carefully, you can keep an inventory of who has gained from your political investments. Quite possibly, the recipient or gainer will perceive that you have anticipated his or her gain through your own actions, and the recipient will feel obliged to help you at a later date. This variant of helping others can be very rewarding to you. The danger, of course, is that the gainer might not realize that your actions were calculated and may not feel indebted to you.

Logrolling

Still another variant of bargaining is the clear-cut case of logrolling in which the involved participants clearly understand that they are acting for mutual gain. In this approach, you should confer with the other participant(s) and plan to combine your resources at one time. Be sure that each of you benefits as a result of this mutual support. Know well in advance that you are helping each other through this temporary coalition. This technique is often used to pass bills and budgets.

Logrolling over time

A slightly more sophisticated approach to the logrolling variant is to help someone attain a legislative or budgetary policy goal under the promise that they will help you later. When engaging in this type of logrolling, you extend the bargaining process over a longer period of time. Still there is mutual gain, but the individuals concerned gain at different points in time. This process can also work the opposite way. You could gain your budgetary or legislative policy goal first and pay back the other participants when they need help in attaining policy goals.

When using the approach of logrolling over time, it is essential that all participants in the bargain be honest and keep their promises. If, for example, you do not keep your half of the bargain, you will surely have gained an enemy, and you will have spoiled your reputation as a credible and honest political figure.

Awarding side payments

An even more sophisticated variant of the logrolling approach is the side payment variety of bargaining. In the side payment variant, you make a bargain in which you trade support on a policy for a promise to help another player on a non-policy goal. For example, by giving someone support for a policy (perhaps a vote), you may be able to get a promise to help in attaining one of your own personal goals (a new position or some critical information). Again the roles may be reversed in this variant. You may trade your support of another participant's personal goal in exchange for his or her promise to help you attain a policy goal at a later point. As in the logrolling over time variant, it is important that you keep your promises when engaging in side payments. Don't get the reputation of not living up to commitments. Unethical behavior will come back to haunt you when you least expect it.

Compromising

A final approach to the bargaining strategy is the art of compromise. This approach involves modifying your goals so as to attain something while allowing another player to make gains by modifying his or her goals. It is a simple matter of finding some mutually acceptable common ground between two divergent positions. The philosophy of compromise is that it is better to get half a loaf than none at all. If you use this approach, you will undoubtedly attain less than you want, but you may get more than you would have by not cooperating.

Successful compromise demands that both participants have accurate pictures or estimates of the other player's real goals. If you overestimate the goals of another person, you will be forced to give up too much in the final compromise. However, if you underestimate their real desires, a compromise will not take place. It is essential that all parties have a clear understanding of each other's basic interests; then this highly experimental technique can yield mutually satisfying results.

7. Depriving others

All variations of bargaining are cooperative in nature. Cooperation, however, is not the only way to achieve your goals. Perhaps you may wish to employ a seventh strategy – depriving others. This uncooperative or antagonistic strategy of deprivation is used on the assumption that it is justifiable to punish those who have prevented you from achieving your goals. It is also felt that it is legitimate to deny another participant one or more of his or her goals if that denial will encourage him or her to cooperate with you in the future. Overall, deprivation is unpleasant, but it can be useful. Be aware, however, that once you deprive another player, you may have permanently defined your relationship to that player in negative terms.

8. Instilling myths and impressions

Our last strategy is the technique of instilling myths and Impressions. This approach emphasizes the manipulation of words so as to make others believe something that is partially or totally false.

One variant of this approach is to use the technique of bluffing. If you have played poker or another card game, you are probably familiar with the bluffing technique. In bluffing, the objective is to create a false impression about your resources and/or capacity to make use of those resources. The advantage of this technique is that you have the chance of achieving some of your goals without really having to take action.

Another variant of the same strategy is the creation of political myths or false interpretations of the actual situation. For example, you can strengthen your own hand by promoting the myth that you are a champion of purity and honesty. At the same time, you can weaken an adversary's position by promoting the myth that he or she is an evil and treacherous enemy of the public interest.

Both bluffing and promoting myths can be extremely effective if your claims are realistic and believable. If other participants feel that your behavior is reliable, they will probably be taken in by this strategy. However, if the other participants suspect that you are lying, they will ignore you or turn against you.

The biggest danger of using these techniques is to go through the agony and embarrassment of having someone call your bluff or openly accuse you of lying. Because of this danger, it is advisable to think carefully before using the myths and impressions strategy. If you do use it, be willing to follow through on your bluffs and be prepared to defend your falsehoods.

Some reminders

As you can see, there are many alternative strategies that can be employed to achieve your goals. Additionally, there is an even greater variety in the actual methods by which you can bring these strategies to life. Perhaps you may rely on one or two strategies, or you may wish to start with some strategies and finish with others. Or it is likely that you might combine or mix these strategies in a creative and personally rewarding manner.

Before you set out to craft your strategies and pursue your goals, you should be aware of a few fine points on effective use of political strategies. These reminders are intended to help you maximize your accomplishments:

1. consider the interests of others;
2. develop a sense of timing;
3. create alternative strategies; and
4. get in the habit of reassessment.

You should always remember to *consider the interest of other participants* in constructing your strategies. Remember that you do not operate in isolation. If your strategies are based on your interests only, you are bound to be ineffective. All the strategies are premised on considering the goals of other participants.

It is also necessary to *develop a sense of timing*. You should develop the talent of selecting the opportune time to implement strategies. If you wait too long, you may end up having to be on the defensive for the duration of the simulation. Similarly, you should not try to accomplish everything at once. The best approach is to wait for the right moment and act decisively.

You will also find that it is useful to *create alternative strategies*. If your original strategies do not succeed, you must be able to fall back on a preplanned second effort. In order to have the capacity to respond to changes in others' goals or strategies, you must develop as many alternatives as possible. With these several alternatives in mind you will be able to move effectively toward your goals.

As a final reminder, it should be emphasized that reassessment is important. You must *make a habit of reassessment*. Constantly ask yourself how you are doing. Are you attaining your goals? Are other people behaving as you expected? Are your strategies working? Might you need to make an adjustment? Should you adjust your priorities? Should you adjust your strategies? Or, should you adjust the rate at which you spend your resources? These questions should always be at the back of your mind. You will find that you will benefit greatly through careful and conscientious assessment.

What You Should Learn

The macro and micro simulations have been created to give you the opportunity to operate on two distinct levels. The first level is the realm of participation in political decision-making. The second level is the realm of analysis of the political process for American national government.

Most of the *Participant's Manual* has been directed at developing your skills in the realm of experience. You have become acquainted with roles, legislation, budgets, court cases, pressures from the political environment and the art of mapping strategies. The last few paragraphs will concentrate on the second level of your learning—*the realm of analysis*; and it will do so by enumerating and examining the basic learning objectives that give theoretical meaning to the participation experience.

These serious political games have been designed to help you come to grips with five important ways of looking at the national political process in the American system. These objectives were introduced in the second chapter of this manual and are reviewed here and discussed in more detail.

1. **Identify the formal and informal players who converge on various issues.**

At the conclusion of the macro or micro simulation, you may be asked to review your *Journal* for the total number of sessions devoted to the exercise. In looking back at that material, list all of the issues that emerged during the course of the game. Second, list the formal (governmental officials) and informal (or non-governmental) players who were involved with each of these issues. Treat governmental officials from foreign countries as informal players in our system.

2. Describe the material and symbolic stakes that motivate players.

Now, take each of these players and speculate about their motivations. What material or tangible goals were they trying to attain in the various issues? What symbolic or emotional objectives were they trying to attain in these cases? Were some of the motives a mixture of material and symbolic? If so, which participants had mixed motives on particular issues?

3. Assess the impact of rules on the decision-making process.

Look back at these various issues and describe how the rules of federalism, separation of powers or checks and balances had an impact on the final decision. Or, what evidence did you see about the operation of rules within our individual political institutions? Did the rules slow down the political process? Did the rules require that multiple branches of government be involved in making decisions?

4. Note the strategies that were employed by various players.

Go back to the various issues and construct an inventory of the types and variations of political strategies that were employed by various participants? To what extent were various strategies used in shaping and making public policy? To what extent were various strategies employed for non-policy purposes?

5. Analyze the results of the political process.

Compare the number of issues that emerged during the simulation with the actual number of policy decisions that were made. Describe these policy decisions and whether these decisions were examples of laws, budgets, orders or opinions. Who gained as a result of these decisions and who lost when these decisions were made? How would you assess each decision in terms of the distribution of costs and benefits? Did this decision concentrate the costs on a relatively small part of the population, or did the decision distribute the cost widely throughout the population? Did this decision concentrate the benefits in the hands of a few, or were the benefits distributed widely?

Parting words

There are many other things that you are bound to learn by participating in **The Game of Politics**©. You will certainly gain a deeper appreciation for the arduous, and sometimes thankless, job of making political decisions. You will undoubtedly come to appreciate your own ability to achieve political goals. Perhaps you will even get to the point of putting some of these basic lessons to work in real life.

If your learning is only limited to the five objectives, you will still have achieved a great deal. You will have developed a clear understanding of how and why political decisions are made. Furthermore, you will have developed an awareness of politics as being an imperfect and experimental process in which humans struggle to achieve their goals while the world around them is constantly changing. That is a lot to learn.

Adamez
Press Secretary for the President (Democrat)

Adamez is from an immigrant family and has had a successful career in journalism. As a reporter, Adamez received considerable recognition for award winning articles on poverty in America. In later years, Adamez became a syndicated newspaper columnist and then was selected as an editor of the Washington Star newspaper. The Millworth administration recruited Adamez as Press Secretary after the President's first Press Secretary developed a problem of credibility with the media.

Adams
Member of House of Representatives from New Hampshire (Democrat)

Adams was a prosecuting attorney who turned a local murder trial, involving a celebrity, into a national sensation. Adams gained so much publicity from the trial that the prosecutor was a natural choice for a vacant seat in the House of Representatives. Adams has a reputation for being very ambitious, yet is seen as quite fair. Representative Adams has been put on the Government Operations Committee of the House and has used that position to help bring government jobs to the congressional district.

Argyle
Associate Justice, United States Supreme Court

After a successful career as a lawyer on Wyoming land use issues, Argyle served in several positions within the state judiciary. At age 45, Judge Argyle was named as the Chief Justice of the Wyoming Supreme Court and then was named to the U.S. District Court. Finally, after another nominee withdrew, Argyle was appointed and confirmed to fill a vacancy on the U.S. Supreme Court. Justice Argyle has written several opinions that have advocated a new balance between the national and state governments.

y

..ited States Senator from California (Democrat)

Avery was elected to the Senate seat after three terms of representing a Sacramento area House district and years of service in the California legislature. Senator Avery has held the Senate seat for more than two terms and chairs the Senate Internal Matters Committee. Republicans have targeted Avery for the coming election. The Senator has been criticized as a Washington insider and is viewed as President "Millworth's Mouthpiece" in the Senate. Representative Zarkasian is expected to challenge Avery.

Ballentine
Attorney, Kirk and Wadowski Law Practice

Ballentine, who grew up in Washington State, graduated from the Harvard Law School just three years ago and had a brief stint as a public defender in Los Angeles. After having built a solid record and even successfully appealing and winning a high-profile case at the U.S. Supreme Court level, Ballentine received several offers from major law firms and recently joined the Kirk and Wadowski Law Practice. Ballentine has also founded a non-profit corporation to find employment opportunities for disabled Americans.

Blake
Member of House of Representatives from Alabama (Republican)

Blake entered the House of Representatives after serving as a state legislator. Blake's quick rise to power was helped when the House incumbent was involved in a sexual scandal. Blake defeated the incumbent by a wide margin. Representative Blake now serves on the House Government Operations Committee, and has a reputation for helping constituents cope with the federal bureaucracy. Local Democrats criticize Blake for not keeping a campaign promise to expand a military installation in the congressional district.

Bogage
Member of House of Representatives from Nebraska (Democrat)

Representative Bogage is a relative newcomer to politics, who first gained public office only six years ago. In a well-financed campaign, Bogage was elected to a seat after the predecessor retired from the position. Bogage comes from a wealthy family that owns several corporate farms. The Representative is a political moderate who is most interested in domestic policies and serves on the Internal Matters Committee. In a surprise upset, Bogage was recently elected as one of the Assistant Minority Leaders of the House.

Carruthers
Senior Partner, Carruthers and Quade Law Practice

Carruthers was a summa cum laude graduate at the University of Michigan and also one of the top graduates of the University of Michigan Law School. After broad experience with other firms, Carruthers joined with another attorney to form the Carruthers and Quade Law Practice in Washington, D.C. The two partners have been in high demand and have represented a wide variety of clients before the U.S. Supreme Court.

Coble
United States Senator from Delaware (Democrat)

Senator Coble comes from a respected political family within the State of Delaware and quickly rose from a seat in the House. Coble serves on the Government Operations Committee, and has earned a reputation in both parties as a quick thinker and problem solver. Senator Coble has been viewed as a political moderate and has been particularly interested in reevaluating the tax system in the United States, and in promoting greater fairness in distributing the tax burden.

Conrad
United States Senator from Virginia (Republican)

Conrad is a superb campaigner, and that accounts for a rapid rise in politics from city council to the U.S. House of Representatives, and then on to the U.S. Senate, in just a dozen years. Currently, Senator Conrad is on the Government Operations Committee. In addition, Conrad serves as an Assistant Minority Leader and is viewed as a potential Minority Leader for the Senate. Conrad is highly respected by both Democrats and Republicans and is seen as a pragmatic conservative.

Culpepper
Member of House of Representatives from Texas (Republican)

Representative Culpepper has won seven congressional elections in an Anglo-Hispanic district outside of San Antonio. Culpepper has risen to the position of Majority Leader of the House of Representatives, and has been encouraged to challenge Representative Villary for the position of Speaker of the House after the next election. In addition to serving as Majority Leader, Culpepper is on the External Matters Committee of the House and is the First Vice Chair of that important committee.

DeWitt
Member of House of Representatives from South Carolina (Republican)

DeWitt was elected to the House of Representatives from a district near Charleston after serving as a local prosecuting attorney and then spending several years in the state legislature. The Representative has been elected to the House for four terms, and is viewed as a strong contender for a Senate seat from South Carolina when it becomes vacant. DeWitt is the Second Vice Chair of both the House Internal Matters as well as the Budget committee. DeWitt's district is a stronghold for KKK activity.

Diggs
Member of House of Representatives from Kansas (Republican)

Diggs began a political career as a county official in western Kansas. Then, Diggs ran for a state legislative seat, and held that office for several years before being appointed to the U.S. House of Representatives following the death of an incumbent. Representative Diggs was reelected by a comfortable margin, has been in the U.S. House for three terms and is a member of the Internal Matters Committee. Diggs is particularly concerned about the decline of the family farm in America and is an advocate for struggling farmers.

Dixon
United State Senator from Tennessee (Democrat)

Dixon is a former Lieutenant Governor of Tennessee who ran for a vacant House seat outside of Knoxville. Representative Dixon held the seat for two terms and then ran for a U.S. Senate seat and was elected by a comfortable margin. Dixon serves on the Senate Government Operations Committee and is the Second Vice Chair of that committee. In addition, Dixon is an Assistant Majority Leader of the Senate. Dixon is viewed as a new type of Democrat and has extensive ties to the business community.

Elmwood
Member of the House of Representatives from Connecticut (Republican)

Representative Elmwood is a medical doctor who ran for Congress in order to help rebuild the health care system in the United States. Elmwood is in a second term in the House and has just published a best selling book entitled Prescription for Medical Reform. Representative Elmwood is a popular speaker at Republican Party fundraisers and is viewed a possible candidate for President at some time in the future. Currently, Elmwood serves on the Government Operations Committee.

Epstein
Associate Justice, United States Supreme Court

Justice Epstein is relatively new to the Supreme Court, but has years of experience on the U.S. Court of Appeals. Epstein grew up, and was educated, in California before practicing criminal law. Epstein eventually became a prosecuting attorney in San Francisco before being selected for the U.S. District Court and then the Court of Appeals. Justice Epstein has been viewed as one of the more moderate members of the Supreme Court.

Estorian
Television Network News Reporter/Analyst

Estorian is a highly respected journalist who has received top ratings from viewers and awards from colleagues. The popular media figure is known for being both objective and willing to dig beneath the surface to get at a good news story. Politicians have mixed feelings about Estorian. They see how the reporter can help them individually through positive publicity. However, they are concerned that Estorian can also hurt them by reporting on controversial or embarrassing matters.

Eubank
United States Senator from Louisiana (Democrat)

Eubank is an ordained minister and a highly respected African-American politician, who has been called "the conscience of the Senate." Senator Eubank has won the last three elections by comfortable margins. Eubank chairs the External Matters Committee and was briefly considered as a possible running mate by President Millworth. Senator Eubank recently received a Nobel Prize for mediating a peace agreement that ended a prolonged territorial war between Peru and Ecuador.

Fenton
United States Senator from Utah (Republican)

Fenton is a retired FBI agent who became a local district attorney for two terms before running for the Senate. Senator Fenton is a first term Senator and has been placed on the External Matters Committee in spite of years of experience in domestic legal issues. Fenton has been a quick learner, and has built a reputation with colleagues as one who works hard and is willing to listen to all points of view. Unfortunately, Fenton's constituents have not been able to see results coming from the Senator's work.

Ferguson
Member of House of Representatives from North Dakota (Republican)

Representative Ferguson has had a career that has taken many twists and turns. Ferguson began as a trial lawyer and county official before running successfully for the state legislature. Ferguson was elected as the Governor of North Dakota, named Secretary of Commerce in a Republican administration and then ran for a vacant seat in the House. Representative Ferguson is now in a sixth term and is Second Vice Chair of the Government Operations Committee. Ferguson is an advocate for small businesses.

Foreman
Member of House Representatives from South Dakota (Democrat)

Representative Foreman entered national politics after a career as a scientist and astronaut. It has always been Foreman's goal to keep the U.S. ahead in science and technology. Representative Foreman fears that we are too comfortable with past achievements and are starting to lose ground to other nations. Foreman is in a fifth term in the House, serves on the Government Operations Committee and has been seeking a position on the important House Budget Committee.

Frock
Foreign and Military Advisor to the President (Democrat)

Frock has had a long and distinguished career as a leading expert on foreign and military issues. Frock is a Harvard Professor of International Relations, and recently hosted an award winning public television series entitled *War and Peace*. The series showed that the new international environment requires the U.S. to be both strong and conciliatory. After Millworth was elected to the White House, the new President asked Frock to take a leave of absence from Harvard to join the new administration.

Galliano
Associate Justice, United States Supreme Court

Galliano served as a Professor of Constitutional Law at Harvard University and established a national reputation as a legal scholar before being appointed to the Supreme Court. Galliano's confirmation hearing was filled with conflict because of some of the law professor's writings on the right to privacy. However, Galliano was finally confirmed as the newest member of the Court.

Gilmore
United State Senator from Vermont (Democrat)

Gilmore is independently wealthy after the sale of a family owned Vermont maple syrup processing company. Senator Gilmore has been elected three times with strong support from university employees and workers from small industrial companies. Gilmore is an environmental advocate and is concerned with the problems that workers face in this era of economic globalization. Representative Gilmore is the Second Vice Chair of the External Matters Committee. Gilmore is an Assistant Majority Leader of the Senate.

Gomez
Member of House of Representatives from New Mexico (Republican)

Gomez, a lawyer, has been elected four times from a district on the outskirts of Santa Fe. Representative Gomez has helped strengthen the Republican Party nationally by increasing the number of Hispanics who register as Republicans. Gomez chairs the House Internal Matters Committee as well as the House Rules Committee. Democrats have targeted Gomez in the next election claiming that Gomez has done very little to help lower-income constituents who live in that House district.

Hardesty
United States Senator from Massachusetts (Democrat)

Senator Hardesty is a major advocate for issues involving children. Senator Hardesty has been in the Senate for two terms and has won each time by narrow margins. The Republican Party has targeted Hardesty in the coming election as being "too liberal" for the people of Massachusetts. Hardesty serves on the External Matters Committee and is the First Vice Chair of that committee. In addition, Hardesty serves on the Senate Budget Committee and is First Vice Chair of that committee.

Hilton
Member of the House of Representatives from Georgia (Democrat)

Hilton was a University President in Georgia prior to being recruited by both parties to run for a vacant seat in suburban Atlanta. Eventually, Hilton decided to run as a Democrat and won both the nomination and general election by a solid margin. Hilton is known as a moderate conservative and has a reputation of being thoughtful and hard driving. Representative Hilton is serving a second term and is on the External Matters Committee. The Representative is building a national reputation in foreign policy.

Inglassi
United States Senator from Illinois (Democrat)

Inglassi established a record as a reform-minded member of the Chicago City Council, and then ran for a seat in the U. S. House of Representatives from a Chicago district. After two terms in the House, Inglassi was elected to the Senate and has established a reputation for increasing the number of federal dollars flowing into Illinois. Inglassi serves on, and is the First Vice Chair of, the Internal Matters Committee of the Senate. In addition, Inglassi chairs the powerful Senate Budget Committee.

Inglewood
Member of House of Representatives from Arizona (Republican)

Representative Inglewood made millions of dollars as a cable television executive before entering politics. Inglewood has developed a national reputation while participating on a Presidential Commission on Economic Growth during a past Republican administration. Currently, Inglewood serves on the Government Operations Committee and is viewed as a moderate conservative on most matters. It is expected that Inglewood will run for an Arizona U.S. Senate seat in the coming election.

Irwin
Chief Justice, United States Supreme Court

Chief Justice Irwin has presided over the Court for more than a decade. Prior to that, Irwin served as an Associate Justice on the U.S. Supreme Court. Originally, Chief Justice Irwin pursued a career in law after graduating from Princeton. It did not take long before Irwin became a Rhode Island state judge and then moved on to the federal judiciary. Irwin has presided over the Supreme Court after a period of internal conflict and is viewed as a consensus-builder.

Jackson
Member of House of Representatives from Nevada (Republican)

Jackson comes from a modest background, but achieved great wealth after developing hardware and software to connect personal computers to the Internet through small satellite dishes. After an early retirement at age 35, Jackson ran for a House seat near Reno to "improve America's technological edge" and won without much opposition. Jackson has been reelected three times. Representative Jackson serves on, and is Second Vice Chair of, both the House External Matters and Rules Committees.

Jones
Television Network News Reporter/Analyst

Jones is viewed as one of the best investigative reporters in the business. Some criticize the reporter for a tabloid style of journalism. However, others have praised Jones for breaking important stories that were being ignored by others. Jones has climbed the ladder of the news business from a small town newspaper in southern Illinois to becoming a major reporter with the New York Courier newspaper. Six months ago, Jones jumped to television journalism and has been an overnight success.

Kelvey
Domestic Advisor to the President (Democrat)

Kelvey was an early supporter when Oregon's Senator Millworth ran for the Presidency. After Millworth was elected, the new President asked Kelvey to be the Domestic Advisor to the President. Kelvey left a safe House seat in Pennsylvania as well as key positions in the House of Representatives to work in the new Millworth Administration. While a member of the House of Representatives, Kelvey was on the House Internal Matters Committee and also was a member of the House Budget Committee.

Kilpatrick
Member of House of Representatives from New Jersey (Republican)

Kilpatrick, a former airlines executive, retired in mid-career and turned to politics to "help America survive in an age of global economic competition." Kilpatrick represents an upper-income suburban district outside of New York City and has been elected five times. The Representative chairs the House External Matters Committee and is First Vice Chair of the House Budget Committee. Kilpatrick was the Republican Vice Presidential candidate in the last election and has strong name recognition among voters.

Kirk
Senior Partner, Kirk and Wadowski Law Practice.

Kirk is a major figure in one of the most sought after law firms in Washington D.C. After growing up in New Hampshire and studying law at Yale University, Kirk established a reputation as one of the most capable young attorneys. Recently, Kirk joined forces with another legal powerhouse and formed the Kirk and Wadowski law practice. The new firm has taken on several high profile cases and represents a variety of clients before the U.S. Supreme Court.

Krumrine
United States Senator from Oklahoma (Democrat)

Krumrine was elected to the Senate after years of climbing the political ladder from local politics. Senator Krumrine has strong support in Oklahoma and has easily won reelection. Currently, Krumrine serves on the Senate External Matters Committee. Krumrine lost a bid for Senate Majority Leader against Senator Meyers of Michigan by a narrow margin. It is rumored that Krumrine will run for Majority Leader against either Senator Gilmore or Senator Dixon after Senator Meyers retires from the job.

Litz
United States Senator from Alaska (Republican)

Litz moved to the Senate after two terms in the House of Representatives. While in the House, Litz established a reputation for advocating environmental concerns while being pro-business. The same skill at balancing environmental and business interests is also evident in the performance of Litz in the Senate. Senator Litz is the ranking minority member of the External Matters and Budget committees. Some experts think that Litz will eventually become Secretary of Defense in a Republican administration.

Lyle
Member of House of Representatives from Arkansas (Democrat)

Lyle comes to politics from a business background. Prior to seeking office, Lyle was the chief executive of a financial services company. Lyle defeated a Republican incumbent member of the House in a long shot race by focusing on the need to start running government like a business. Representative Lyle has been reelected twice and is extremely popular back home in the district. The Representative has been quite content to concentrate on the Government Operations Committee and the Rules Committee.

Marrow
Associate Justice, United States Supreme Court

Justice Marrow originally came from Minnesota and was appointed to the Court after distinguished service as Attorney General of both Minnesota and the United States. Marrow has served on the Court longer than any of the other current justices. During Marrow's tenure, the justice established a reputation for high principles and has often taken the role as the devil's advocate in Court deliberations. Marrow's opinions have helped shape several legal precedents, and many say that Justice Marrow has helped stabilize the Court during a time of ideological struggle. It is rumored that Marrow will retire at the end of this term.

Merkle
Member of House of Representatives from Rhode Island (Democrat)

Representative Merkle moved from a career as a social worker to political activism. After a brief stint on the city council of Providence, Merkle ran for the House of Representatives and emerged as the winner among eight primary election candidates. Merkle currently serves on the House External Matters Committee. Representative Merkle has been gaining considerable support from recent immigrant citizens as well as the business community. Merkle seems like a likely contender for a Senate seat.

Meyers
United States Senator from Michigan (Democrat)

Senator Meyers has a solid electoral base in Michigan and has held office for four terms, after serving for three terms in the House. Meyers is Majority Leader of the Senate and has kept Senate Democrats together on controversial issues. Senator Meyers was very helpful in advancing the programs of President Millworth in the last session. Meyers is also the First Vice Chair of the Government Operations Committee and the Second Vice Chair of the Budget Committee. It is expected that Senator Meyers will retire at the end of this term.

Miller
Member of House of Representatives from Wyoming (Republican)

Miller was a young intelligence officer during World War II whose emphasis on detail saved the lives of thousands of U.S. soldiers during the U.S. invasion at Normandy. Miller entered politics in Wyoming, was elected to the U.S. House of Representatives in the early 1970s and has years of service on the External Matters Committee. Democrats criticize Miller for accomplishing very little and claim that the Representative is just too old for the job. Representative Miller completed the Boston Marathon this past year.

Millworth
President of the United States (Democrat)

After two terms as a Senator from Oregon, Millworth ran for the office of President and promised "new ideas for new times." The Oregon Senator was elected by a narrow margin. During the first year of the new administration, Millworth had difficulty in getting a program through the Congress. The President had strong support from the Democratic majority in the Senate but was stopped by the Republican dominated House of Representatives. Millworth is the first President to get a divorce while in the White House.

Nedwick
Member of House of Representatives from Iowa (Republican)

Nedwick was a former Mayor of Des Moines and was appointed to a seat in the House following the death of the incumbent. Representative Nedwick then won the seat in two closely contested elections. Nedwick is an Assistant Majority Leader of the House and serves on the House Internal Matters Committee. Nedwick is attempting to establish a positive track record to gain financial contributions. The Representative wants to win by a much larger margin in the coming election against a popular Democrat.

Nunelly
United States Senator from Maine (Republican)

Nunelly rose quickly in politics over a twenty year period from local government to state legislature to U.S. House of Representatives, and finally to the U.S. Senate. In the recent contests for Senate, Nunelly won by a very small margin and is anticipating a tough reelection. Democrats have criticized Senator Nunelly for not taking a clear position on the debate between logging interests and environmentalists. Nunelly serves on the Internal Matters Committee and is an Assistant Minority Leader.

Odenton
Associate Justice, United States Supreme Court

Justice Odenton grew up in Mississippi and comes from a very modest background. However, Odenton excelled in school and eventually graduated from law school in Florida. Odenton specialized in cases concerned with equal opportunity and also taught in law schools. Eventually Odenton became Dean of the Law School at Duke University. When a vacancy came up for the Supreme Court, Odenton was a first choice and was nominated and confirmed without any problems. Justice Odenton is the only African-American on the Court.

Ogura
United States Senator from Hawaii (Democrat)

Senator Ogura is a Japanese-American who rose from the position of local government judge to the House of Representatives and then on to the U. S. Senate. The popular Senator has developed a reputation for being quite independent. Ogura is viewed as a strong possibility for United States Supreme Court. However, there are concerns that the Democrats would lose the seat to the Republicans if Ogura were appointed to the Supreme Court. Senator Ogura chairs the Government Operations Committee.

Olney
United States Senator from Missouri (Democrat)

Representative Olney comes with years of experience in the Missouri State Legislature, has been in the U.S. Senate for three terms, and is Second Vice Chair of the Internal Matters Committee. Olney represents a district in southwest Missouri that has changed from rural to suburban in a short period of time. New suburban residents are angry that their communities have lost their rural character while their property taxes are rising to support new roads and schools. Republicans have targeted Olney in the next election.

Pascal
Member of House of Representatives from North Carolina (Republican)

Pascal is the former Governor of North Carolina who lost in a bid for United States Senate. Then, Pascal won a House seat and has been reelected several times. Representative Pascal is a member of the External Matters Committee and is known as a supporter of a strong military. Pascal has been particularly concerned with America's conciliatory approach to foreign governments under the Millworth Administration. According to Pascal, America should only bargain from a position of strength.

Prescott
Member of House of Representatives from Mississippi (Republican)

Representative Prescott, a former high school principal, has had a distinguished career in state and local, as well as national, politics. Prescott rose to the position of Speaker of the House of the Mississippi legislature and is rumored to be seeking a similar role at the national level. Representative Prescott now serves on both the Government Operations Committee and the Rules Committee. Prescott is seen as a political conservative but is willing to compromise to reach agreement.

Quade
Senior Partner, Carruthers and Quade Law Practice

Quade is the other half of the highly respected law firm of Carruthers and Quade. Ten years ago, Quade, who originally came from New Mexico and is a top graduate of the University of Chicago Law School, received national recognition by being the youngest lawyer to argue and win a case before the U. S. Supreme Court. It was not too long afterward that Quade joined Carruthers to form one of the top law firms in Washington D.C.

Reese
United States Senator from Colorado (Republican)

Reese left the position of a television anchor in Denver to run for the U.S. Senate and won by a very comfortable margin. Senator Reese has held the seat for two terms and is a rising star within the Republican Party. Reese is very skilled at using the media to gain publicity. Senator Reese serves on the Government Operations Committee in the Senate and also serves as ranking minority member of that committee. Reese is also a member of the powerful Senate Budget Committee.

Rifkin
Attorney, Carruthers and Quade Law Practice

Since joining the Carruthers and Quade Law Practice, Rifkin has established a reputation as an attorney who really knows how to win at the Supreme Court level. Rifkin was born in North Dakota, graduated from high school at age sixteen, then went on and became an honors student at Syracuse University in New York. After law school and two years of service teaching on an Indian reservation, Rifkin was directly recruited to join the Carruthers and Quade Law Practice.

Rourke
Vice President of the United States (Democrat)

Rourke represented a House of Representatives district in North Carolina and was on the External Matters Committee before running unsuccessfully for the Democratic Party nomination for President. The struggle between Millworth and Rourke was particularly bitter and there were many charges and countercharges. After Millworth received the nomination, Millworth offered the Vice Presidential spot to Rourke in order to balance the ticket and bring Rourke's valuable military and foreign policy credentials to the campaign.

Ruby
Foreign and Military Advisor to the President (Democrat)

Ruby has lived in northern Virginia for many years and has taught graduate courses in military affairs at American University in Washington D.C. Ruby has been an international adviser to three Presidents and has a reputation as a reliable negotiator with foreign governments. Ruby has written extensively on military preparedness and is an advocate of a strong military. Professor Ruby has been said to also have close ties with the Central Intelligence Agency and is an expert on espionage.

Simon
Member of House of Representatives from New York State (Democrat)

Simon taught Educational Psychology for 15 years at Columbia University and served on several national presidential advisory committees, before being recruited into politics. In a first attempt, Simon defeated an incumbent Republican from Long Island. Representative Simon is the ranking minority member on the Government Operations Committee in the House and is also the Minority Leader of the House of Representatives. Simon is considered a valuable ally of President Millworth.

Simowitz
United States Senator from Maryland (Democrat)

Simowitz began a career in politics after years of managing nonprofit organizations. Simowitz moved quickly from a seat on a school board in the Baltimore area to the state legislature. Then, Simowitz ran for and won a place in the House of Representatives before running for the United States Senate. Senator Simowitz has held that office for one term and serves on the Internal Matters Committee. Republican critics say that Simowitz is far too liberal, even for Maryland, and too allied with Israel.

Stevenson
Associate Justice, United States Supreme Court

Justice Stevenson grew up in Texas and has demonstrated a streak of Texas-style independence on the Court. When appointed and confirmed, it was felt that Stevenson was going to be a "strict constructionist" and not stretch the Constitution to fit contemporary situations. Instead, Stevenson has moved back and forth between a literal interpretation of the Constitution and a more expansive view. Stevenson had years of experience in the federal courts before being appointed to the Supreme Court.

Timkin
Member of House of Representatives from Montana (Republican)

Timkin built a successful law practice in the city of Billings before entering into state politics. After several terms as a state legislator, Timkin ran for and won the office of Lieutenant Governor. Serving in that office gave Timkin enough of a reputation to seek and win a seat in the U.S. House of Representatives. Representative Timkin serves on the House External Matters Committee and is an Assistant Majority Leader. Economic stagnation within Timkin's district has posed problems for reelection.

Tracey
United States Senator from Florida (Republican)

After a successful career as a real estate developer in the St. Petersburg area, Tracey entered politics to help promote policies that were friendly to the business community, "the economic blood supply for the nation." Tracey is the Minority Leader of the Senate and ranking minority member of the Internal Matters Committee. Tracey is viewed as a possible Senate Majority leader if the Republicans regain the Senate. There are also many rumors that Tracey is seeking the Republican nomination for President.

Ulman
Member of House of Representatives from Idaho (Republican)

Representative Ulman is a former mining company executive who ran for Congress in order to bring new ideas to Washington D.C. Since arriving on the national scene, Ulman has established a reputation as somewhat of a political maverick. Representative Ulman has been elected for five terms by increasing margins and is very popular in the Congressional district. Ulman serves on the External Matters Committee and has recently been appointed to the House of Representatives Budget Committee.

Ulmont
Associate Justice, United States Supreme Court

Ulmont stands in the middle of the Supreme Court in several respects. Four of the justices were appointed before Ulmont and the other four were appointed after. Moreover, Ulmont tends to be the moderate justice in terms of positions on issues. However, Ulmont often surprises colleagues by sometimes taking bold positions on issues and siding with one of the liberal or conservative factions. Ulmont brings years of judicial experience from Illinois and the federal judiciary to the Supreme Court.

Ulsterick
Member of House of Representatives from Wisconsin (Democrat)

Ulsterick was a University of Wisconsin Professor of International Relations and is an expert on military policy. Ulsterick ran for a vacant U.S. House of Representatives position and won with the backing of the University community. Representative Ulsterick is now in a third term and has been placed on the Budget Committee and External Matters Committee. It is expected that Representative Ulsterick will become a key player in helping build legislative support for the President's foreign policy initiatives.

Unger
Member of House of Representatives from Washington State (Democrat)

After serving as Governor of Washington state, Unger formed a nonprofit organization, XCHANGE, to promote international understanding through foreign exchange programs for young professionals in a variety of fields. Unger was later convinced to run for a vacant House seat in the Seattle area. Representative Unger has been reelected twice and is the ranking minority member of both the External Matters and the Rules committees within the House. Unger has been viewed as a future presidential candidate.

Vakarios
Member of House of Representatives from Ohio (Republican)

Representative Vakarios began as a reform-minded Mayor of Cleveland and served in that capacity for three terms. Vakarios won a U.S. House of Representatives seat quite easily when a vacancy occurred. Vakarios has established a reputation for being tough on crime. As Mayor of Cleveland, Vakarios increased the size and effectiveness of the police force and brought down the crime rate. Representative Vakarios has also taken a tough position on crime in the Internal Matters Committee and on the floor of the House.

Villary
Member of House of Representatives from Indiana (Republican)

Villary has a very safe seat south of Indianapolis and has been reelected seven times. Representative Villary has held the position of Speaker of the House for the past six years and is presently the First Vice Chair of the Internal Matters Committee in the House. Villary had major responsibility for blocking President Millworth's program in the last session. Yet, some Republicans are becoming disappointed with Villary's leadership and are leaning towards Culpepper, Nedwick or Prescott.

Wadowski
Senior Partner, Kirk and Wadowski Law Practice

Wadowski is a tough-minded New York City lawyer who has played a major role in several Supreme Court cases, particularly since helping create the law firm of Kirk and Wadowski. Combining a Columbia Law School degree with knowledge learned in the streets of New York has resulted in an attorney who has been called one of the best lawyers in America. In addition to a legal career, Wadowski also has a national reputation for growing orchids.

Williams
Member of House of Representatives from Kentucky (Republican)

Representative Williams has held the same seat outside Louisville for nearly 20 years and has been very successful in bringing public works projects to the district, in part, because Williams chairs the House Government Operations Committee and is First Vice Chair of the Rules Committee. The Representative's victory margin has been slipping in the past three elections. Democrats have targeted Williams in the next election and plan to run a candidate with positive name recognition who will emphasize social issues.

Wright
Member of House of Representatives from Oregon (Republican)

Wright lost in a bitter Senate race to Millworth before Millworth was elected as President of the United States. Two years later, Wright was elected to the House of Representatives and has been reelected by comfortable margins. Currently, Wright has been assigned to the Internal Matters Committee of the House of Representatives and has been building a reputation for tax incentive proposals aimed at environmentally friendly businesses. Wright advocates cooperation between business and government.

Yardley
Associate Justice, United States Supreme Court

Justice Yardley comes from one of the most highly regarded families in Georgia. After college and a year of volunteer service, Yardley went on to law school at Wake Forest University and graduated at the top of the class. Yardley was appointed to the Supreme Court after years of experience as a judge and as Director of the FBI. Yardley has established a positive reputation on the Supreme Court, and the Justice's legal opinions have served as the foundations for many new precedents.

Yarmolinski
Member of House of Representatives from Pennsylvania (Democrat)

Yarmolinski has been elected several times from a safe city/suburban district in the Pittsburgh area. The Representative has strong support from organized labor, and works to have government meet the needs of ordinary people. Yarmolinski is the ranking minority member of the Internal Matters Committee in the House of Representatives and is also ranking minority member of the House Budget Committee. Representative Yarmolinski is known for being highly principled and for being a tough negotiator.

Young
Domestic Advisor to the President (Democrat)

Young comes from the State of Montana and has a reputation of being a tough, highly energetic politician. Young entered political life by working on the campaign of a U.S. Senator from Montana, then became the main speechwriter for the Senator. Young left that position to join the campaign of Senator Millworth from Oregon who was running for President. After Millworth was elected, the President asked Young to join the administration and help achieve the administration's legislative agenda.

Zahn
Member of the House of Representatives from Minnesota (Democrat)

Representative Zahn is a former county prosecuting attorney and Minnesota Attorney General who ran for a House seat after the incumbent retired. Zahn now serves on the Internal Matters Committee and was almost selected as an Assistant Minority Leader of the House of Representatives. Representative Zahn is viewed as a highly skillful politician, and seems destined for higher office. Zahn is a political moderate and has established a reputation in domestic policy over three terms in Congress.

Zarkasian
Member of House of Representatives from California (Republican)

After serving as Mayor of Pasadena, Zarkasian challenged the incumbent and was elected to the House of Representatives on a pro-family platform. In the current session of the House, Zarkasian serves on the House Government Operations Committee and is the First Vice Chair of that committee. Zarkasian is also on the Budget Committee and serves as Chair of that committee. Zarkasian is viewed as a strong candidate for the United States Senate seat held by California Senator Avery.

Zepp
Member of House of Representatives from West Virginia (Democrat)

Zepp's father was a coal miner who died in a mining accident. Zepp was the youngest of eight children and has always been highly ambitious. After college, Zepp was elected to the state legislature and eventually went on to become Governor of West Virginia. Governor Zepp initiated a number of programs to diversify the West Virginia economy. Zepp was elected to the U.S. House of Representatives, is serving on the Internal Matters Committee and has been selected as an Assistant Minority Leader.

101 U.S. PARTICIPATION IN OLYMPICS
Referred to External Matters Committee

In order to promote fair athletic competition, the United States government will guarantee that American participants in the summer or winter Olympic games have amateur status and have not received any public funds for training or expenses. In exchange for this guarantee, the United States expects foreign governments to abide by these same restrictions.

In the event that foreign governments refuse to abide by the amateur status rule, then, the United States will explore the creation of an Amateur Olympic Competition with summer and winter games. Competitions will be permanently hosted in the U.S.A. at the same time periods as the traditional Olympic games.

Fiscal Note: $0 unless new games are created

102 NATIONAL ADOPTION CENTER
Referred to Internal Matters Committee

In order to promote the well-being of children and provide them with greater opportunities, the national government creates a National Adoption Center in the Department of Health and Human Services. This Center will work in cooperation with state government social service agencies, will maintain a database and will provide funding to assist in the placement of children who have been born out of wedlock, abandoned or removed from unfit parents. The center would also pay costs associated with placing a child in a different state.

Fiscal Note: $2.5 Billion annual expenditure

103 INSURANCE AND MENTAL ILLNESS
Referred to Government Operations Committee

In order to provide health care for all citizens, the national government prohibits denial of a claim or limitation of services to those who have some form of mental illness. Insurance companies will use the same standards in evaluating mental illness claims as they do physical illness claims. Patients may bring lawsuits if they believe they were denied treatment because they had a mental illness.

Fiscal Note: $0

104 COMPREHENSIVE PROFILE FOR FOREIGN VISITORS
Referred to External Matters Committee

In order to protect our nation against the threat of terrorism, all foreign visitors will be required to provide a complete profile each time they plan to visit the United States.

Such profiles will be furnished at American embassies or consulates in the visitors' home country. Each profile will include a complete personal history, fingerprints, genetic samples as well as positive letters of recommendations from three American citizens.

Information from these profiles will be entered into a database and may be used for investigative purposes.

Fiscal Note: $ 2 Billion annual expenditure

105 WEIGHT LOSS FRAUD
Referred to Internal Matters Committee

In order to protect consumers against fraudulent claims, the Federal Trade Commission prohibits the use of the broadcast and cable media to make exaggerated claims about weight loss that cannot be substantiated by medical research. Moreover, the Commission will prohibit advertisement of weight loss claims that have had negative effects on health. The Commission has the authority to order that such advertisements be withdrawn.

Fiscal Note: $2 Million annual expenditure

106 CAMPAIGN REFORM
Referred to Government Operations Committee

In an effort to reform the campaign funding process, individuals will be limited to a $5,000 contribution per year to the campaign of a specific candidate. Candidates will not be able to receive additional funds from political parties, political action committees or other organizations. Candidates may spend no more than $100 per potential voter in the election for which they are campaigning.

Fiscal Note: $0

107 RESPONSE TO HUMAN RIGHTS ABUSES
Referred to External Matters Committee

In an effort to promote human rights, an Assistant Secretary for Human Rights will be established within the United States State Department. This official will monitor cases of human rights abuses in other countries and recommend specific responses to the Secretary of State and to the President. Such responses can include diplomatic protests, trade sanctions, additional economic actions, as well as military responses.

By creating this position, the United States declares that documented human rights abuses constitute crimes against humanity and will be met with an assured response by our government.

Fiscal Note: $250 Thousand annual expenditure

108 SUPPORT FOR CAREGIVERS
Referred to Internal Matters Committee

In an effort to support families in times of need, the national government establishes a Family Caregiver Fund that allows private companies, non-profit organizations and government agencies to continue compensating employees when they are serving as caregivers for a family member.

After an employee is authorized to take a Caregiver Leave based on a physician recommendation, the employer will continue to pay all wages and benefits to the employee for up to one calendar year and then bring the employee back to their old position or a better position at the conclusion of the Caregiver Leave. The employer will be compensated for these expenses out of a national Family Caregiver Fund.

The employee is limited to no more than three one-year leaves of absence in any five-year period.

Fiscal Note: $ 15 Billion annual expenditure

109 NATIONAL SALES TAX, NATIONAL DEBT
Referred to Government Operations Committee

In order to prevent future generations from having to pay back a large public debt, the national government will institute a 3 percent National Sales Tax based on all goods and services that are sold within the United States. This tax will be used to accelerate payments on the national debt. This tax will not exceed 3 percent and will be removed at such time that the national debt has been eliminated.

Fiscal Note: $170 Billion annual revenue and $15 Million annual collection expenses

110 PAYMENTS TO THE UNITED NATIONS
Referred to External Matters Committee

In an effort to solidify the financial base of the United Nations, the United States commits itself to annual payments equal to .000001 percent of the annual gross domestic product of the American economy. In reconstituting its economic commitment to the United Nations, the United States seeks to set an example to other nations to make a similar commitment to the international organization and its work.

Fiscal Note: $1.5 Billion annual expenditure

111 FAMILY LEAVE
Referred to Internal Matters Committee

In order to support families, the government of the United States guarantees that all employees of organizations of 50 or more employees have the right to take an unpaid leave of one year from work for child rearing or family illness. This leave may be taken during a period of 365 days or be divided up between several occurrences over a five-year period. Employees will be guaranteed the opportunity to regain their positions or similar positions upon their return to the workplace.

Fiscal Note: $0

112 NATIONAL MINUTE OF SILENCE
Referred to Government Operations Committee

In an effort to raise the standards of morality within the United States, the national government will establish a National Minute of Silence on the first Monday of June. Services will take place at 1:00 p.m. Eastern Time. All national, state and local government offices will be closed and companies that have contractual relationships with the national government will also be closed. Americans will be invited to join their government officials in silent meditation.

Fiscal Note: $0

113 TARIFFS ON U.S. GOODS AND SERVICES
Referred to External Matters Committee

In an effort to promote free trade, the United States commits itself to counteract unfair trade practices by other nations. Through this act, the President of the United States is required to authorize tariffs on a foreign government's goods and services as a measured response to that foreign government's tariffs on U.S. goods and services. Such an assured response is designed to discourage foreign governments from protecting inefficient foreign industries.

Fiscal Note: $3 Million annual expenditure

114 HIGH SPEED RAIL TRAVEL
Referred to Internal Matters Committee

In an effort to promote greater fuel efficiency in the transportation of goods and passengers, the United States will provide direct assistance to private railroad corporations to construct and maintain a high-speed rail system that can serve the continental United States. As in the case of interstate highways and airports, the federal government will provide initial funds to build the infrastructure that is needed to link major cities throughout the United States. The private corporations will be responsible for maintaining the rail system.

Fiscal Note: $7 Billion annual expenditure

115 RESOURCE OWNERSHIP
Referred to Government Operations Committee

In order to promote responsible management of valuable resources, the national government will assume complete ownership of all resources on or below public or private lands. No private company may claim to own or attempt to extract resources from lands controlled by the national government. However, such companies may exploit resources under special contractual relationships with the national government.

Fiscal Note: $100 Billion annual revenue

116 WORLD COURT DECISIONS
Referred to External Matters Committee

In order to demonstrate support for the World Court as well as the concept of international justice, the United States agrees that it will obey any adverse World Court decisions in the event that the United States is a party to an international legal action. This commitment to the World Court is for a period of five years and will be withdrawn if other nations decline to obey World Court decisions.

Fiscal Note: dependent on size of potential lawsuits

117 OFFSHORE PRISONS
Referred to Internal Matters Committee

In order to adapt to the increasing number of prisoners in state prisons as well as the national prisons, the national government will convert decommissioned naval vessels into prisons that can be set afloat off the coast of the United States. These ships will be designed for medium to maximum-security prisoners and will be able to accommodate both federal and state inmates. These offshore prison ships will be leased to private companies who will guarantee prison security on a contractual basis. Private companies will bid for the right to manage these offshore prisons.

Fiscal Note: $10 Billion annual expenditure

118 DIGITAL IMPLANTS FOR PRISONERS AND PAROLEES
Referred to Government Operations Committee

In order to aid law enforcement officials in their investigations, the national government will place digital implants under the skin of all current federal prisoners and parolees through minor surgery. This digital implant will emit a unique signal (with a 20 mile range) that can be used to locate these individuals in the event that police wish to question them about a criminal case. New implants will be installed every four years.

State governments may participate in this program if they use the same type of digital implants and tracking system as well as pay for their own program costs.

A national database will be constructed to organize this information and enable federal, state and local police officials to speed up the process of locating suspects.

Fiscal Note: $ 11 Billion annual expenditure

119 SPACE PROBE
Referred to External Matters Committee

In order to further the space program, the United States government authorizes the National Aeronautics and Space Administration to design, construct, test and eventually launch a space probe that can explore our solar system and beyond for general and commercial purposes. This project is designed to preserve the role of the United States as the leading nation in space exploration and maintain world leadership in technological development.

Fiscal Note: $75 Billion annual expenditure

120 NATIONAL HIGHER EDUCATION CURRICULUM
Referred to Internal Matters Committee

In order to promote the high quality and transferability of college and university courses, a national higher education curriculum will be designed by the United States Department of Education. The Department will survey existing and future courses and develop common course numbers and course descriptions. Colleges and universities will use these numbers and descriptions in their catalogs, advertisements and records. All new courses must be approved and numbered by the Department of Education.

Fiscal Note: $200 Million annual expenditure

121 GENDER TESTING
Referred to Government Operations Committee

In order to prohibit gender selection by parents, no doctor or other medical professional may use diagnostic tests to determine an unborn child's gender. Such tests constitute a violation of the privacy rights of the unborn. Those who desire to have a child of a certain gender will, however, be authorized to give up their unwanted child after birth for adoption.

Fiscal Note: $0

122 NORTH AMERICAN NATURAL RESOURCES PRESERVATION ACT
Referred to External Matters Committee
Ratification by Senate required

In order to protect the environment, the United States commits itself to working with Canada and Mexico to preserve natural resources where the actions of one nation have an adverse effect on the natural resources of a neighbor. The U.S. Department of the Interior will explore areas of common concern with the natural resource departments of the Canadian and Mexican governments. Reasonable efforts should be made to coordinate national policies to preserve scarce natural resources.

Fiscal Note: $1 Billion annual expenditure

123 MINIMUM WAGE INCREASE AND CONSUMER PRICE INDEX
Referred to Internal Matters Committee

In order to help low wage employees keep up with inflation, the United States Department of Labor will adjust the minimum wage at the conclusion of each calendar year based on changes in the consumer price index. This automatic adjustment process will be used instead of periodic legislative adjustments to the minimum wage. Minimum wages will not be reduced in the event of declining cost of living.

Fiscal Note: $0

124 VOTER REGISTRATION
Referred to Government Operations Committee

In an effort to increase public participation in elections, any person who has attained the status of citizen either through birth or naturalization will automatically be registered to vote. This registration will not be affected by change in residence. Individual voter registration certificates will be issued by the Federal Elections Commission and will be available in U. S. post offices or overseas American embassies to individuals possessing birth certificates or citizenship papers.

Fiscal Note: $25 Million annual expenditure

125 REFUGEES AND IMMIGRATION QUOTAS
Referred to External Matters Committee

In order to stabilize immigration into the United States, the Immigration and Naturalization Service will maintain the present quota system for immigration from foreign nations. However, the Immigration and Naturalization Service will modify each nation's quota by admitting economic refugees as well as political refugees. Moreover, the quota for each nation will be limited to adult immigrants who possess occupational skills that are in demand in the United States. Children of immigrants will be admitted without any occupational requirement and will be counted towards a specific nation's quota.

Fiscal Note: $5 Million annual expenditure

126 ENTERTAINMENT RATING SYSTEM AND TAXATION
Referred to Internal Matters Committee

In order to promote moral standards, The Federal Communications Commission shall classify all entertainment delivered by movie, television, tape, cassette, disk or other means according to a numeric scale prior to release. A score of 0 indicates that there is no sexual content or violence contained in the item. A score of 1 indicates that there is some sexual content or violence contained in the item. A score of 2 indicates that there is significant sexual content or violence contained in the item. The manufacturer of the entertainment item will be assessed a tax that is equal to 25 percent of production costs times the numeric value of the item. This tax will be included in the selling price of the item.

Fiscal Note: $30 Million annual revenue

127 SIMPLIFIED TAX SYSTEM
Referred to Government Operations Committee

In order to bring clarity to the tax system, there will be a single rate of 12 percent of all income for the federal income tax. Gross income will be reported and be subject to the 12 percent tax rate.

All means to reduce income tax liability, such as deductions, exemptions, allowances or credits will no longer be a part of the tax system.

Fiscal Note: $55 Billion annual revenue

128 USE OF THE MILITARY IN WAR AGAINST DRUGS
Referred to External Matters Committee

In an effort to protect the health and safety of the American people, the United States declares war against the production and distribution of illegal drugs. This declaration enables the President to deploy the military forces of the United States to counteract and defeat those individuals, organizations and nations that benefit from the narcotics trade. The President can send American forces to any location within the borders of the United States as well as foreign countries to achieve this objective.

Fiscal Note: $2 Billion annual expenditure

129 NATIONAL SCHOOL STANDARDS
Referred to Internal Matters Committee

In an effort to raise the level of academic preparation for American public high school graduates, the United States Department of Education will establish a set of new national educational standards and a one-day exit examination to measure graduates' achievement of those standards. Local school systems can volunteer to give the examination and will be eligible to receive $25 per student taking the test as well as another $25 for each student who has achieved all the national standards. The United States Department of Education will publish an annual report ranking each school based on the percentage of graduates achieving each national standard.

Fiscal Note: $5.5 Billion annual expenditure

130 ABORTION BAN
Referred to Government Operations Committee

In the interest of preserving the lives of the unborn, no person may perform an abortion within the United States or its territories except in cases where the mother has been raped or is in medical danger because of the pregnancy. Any person performing an illegal abortion will be tried for premeditated murder as a federal crime and will be subject to appropriate punishments.

Fiscal Note: $2 Million annual expenditure

131 ORGANIZATION OF WORLD BANK, WTO AND IMF
Referred to External Matters Committee

In order to balance the goals of world economic stability, economic growth and the needs of less developed nations, the United States resolves and urges other member nations to also resolve that the World Bank, the World Trade Organization (WTO) and International Monetary Fund (IMF) be reorganized.

Each organization would have an executive committee and staff to carry out the financial policies that are prescribed by the governing bodies of each organization.

The governing bodies of the World Bank, the WTO and the IMF would each be comprised of three chambers. In one chamber of each organization, each member nation would have one vote regardless of its economic resources or population size. In the second chamber of each organization, the votes allowed to each member nation would be based on national wealth (1 vote for every $1 Billion of gross domestic product). In the third chamber of each organization, the votes of each member nation would be based on population size (1 vote fore every 10 million people).

All three chambers must be in agreement before the WTO or IMF could carry out any action.

Fiscal Note: $ 3 Million annual expenditure

132 HUMAN ORGAN COMMERCE
Referred to Internal Matters Committee

In order to meet the growing shortages of material for transplanting human organs, the Department of Health and Human Services will license companies to purchase and sell such organs. These companies may contract with individuals in the United States or other countries to harvest their organs at the time of their deaths. These companies may then surgically remove the organs and pay the contracted amount, as well as expenses for cremation of the remains. Such companies may sell harvested organs in order to meet critical needs for organ transplants. The Department of Health and Human Services may withdraw a company's license if it determines that the company is distributing diseased organs.

Fiscal Note: $5 Billion annual revenue from licenses

133 OPEN MEETINGS
Referred to Government Operations Committee

Out of the need for public oversight of government decisions, all official and unofficial meetings of the legislative, executive and judicial branches of the United States will be open to public scrutiny. Private citizens or the media will be permitted in any meeting at any level of decision-making.

Fiscal Note: $0

134 NUCLEAR WEAPONS
Referred to External Matters Committee
Ratification by Senate Required

In order to promote world peace, the United States will dismantle its arsenal of nuclear weapons over the next 20 years. An equal number of weapons will be dismantled each year during this time period. The least sophisticated weapons will be phased out first. The United States will allow other nations to inspect our facilities for the purpose of verifying that nuclear weapons are being dismantled at the appropriate rate. These disarmament actions are contingent upon similar actions by other nuclear powers.

Fiscal Note: $10 Million annual expenditure

135 TELEVISED EXECUTIONS
Referred to Internal Matters Committee

The Federal Bureau of Prisons may authorize television coverage of executions. Television production companies will be charged a fee to tape specific executions and will be able to distribute these programs on broadcast television, cable television, videotape or other format. Such programs must also include anti-crime messages. Funds earned from television coverage of executions will be used for law enforcement purposes at the national level of government.

Fiscal Note: $3 Billion annual revenue

136 DIGITAL BROADCAST SPECTRUM
Referred to Government Operations Committee

In order to create greater public benefit from new technologies, the Federal Communications Commission will auction all the frequencies on the broadcast spectrum for digital television. Successful bidders will be able to lease digital frequencies for a five-year period after which the next auction will take place. All funds generated from this auction will be placed in the national government budget and can be used for any purpose.

Companies that attain ownership of frequencies through the auction will still be subject to other federal regulations.

Fiscal Note: $9 Billion revenue for five years

137 WORLD TRADE ORGANIZATION AND FREE TRADE
Referred to External Matters Committee

In an effort to promote free trade among nations, the United States will provide a five-year timetable for the World Trade Organization to achieve complete free trade between all member nations through the elimination of tariffs. The United States will suspend trading relationships with any World Trade Organization member nation that retains tariffs after the five-year period.

Fiscal Note: $0

138 FEDERAL SUPPORT FOR SPECIAL EDUCATION PROGRAMS
Referred to Internal Matters Committee

In order to allow local school systems to dedicate their resources for the curriculum that serves the greatest number of students, the national government's Department of Education will provide construction, material and personnel funding for costly special education programs. These programs will be retained at the local level but will be separated from the rest of the local educational program. The students in special education will be offered those aspects of an overall educational program from which they can benefit. However, the special education students will not be expected to complete the regular curriculum.

Fiscal Note: $12 Billion annual expenditure

139 BAN ON AFFIRMATIVE ACTION PROGRAMS
Referred to Government Operations Committee

In an effort to prevent patterns of reverse discrimination, no government agency, school or private organization can impose a personnel or student recruitment plan that favors any minority group. All hiring and other selection processes will be based exclusively on credentials. Race, gender or other such factors will not be taken into account.

Individuals who believe they have been discriminated against because of past affirmative action policies may bring suit for loss of income.

Fiscal Note: $0

140 REINSTITUTING THE MILITARY DRAFT
Referred to External Matters Committee

In order to promote military readiness and involve citizens in defense efforts, the Selective Service System will reinstate the military draft to recruit personnel for the United States Army. Local draft boards will, depending on Army personnel needs, employ a lottery-type system to select male and female draftees for two-year periods of service. The only deferments that will be granted will be for critical family circumstances, disability and proven moral objection to military service.

Fiscal Note: $ 1 Billion annual expenditure

141 LIMITATION ON LEGAL FEES IN LAWSUITS
Referred to Internal Matters Committee

In an effort to reduce the amount of litigation, lawyers may not receive more than 10 percent of the award in a civil trial involving litigants who are from different states. This limitation does not apply to lawsuits involving litigants within the same state, except in those situations in which one of the litigants moved across state boundaries after the suit was filed.

Fiscal Note: $0

142 INDEPENDENT VOTERS AND PRIMARY ELECTIONS
Referred to Government Operations Committee

In order to promote more public participation in the electoral process, each state will revise its election laws so that independent voters can vote in primary elections for candidates of any political party.

Independent voters may continue to vote for candidates of any party during the general election.

Fiscal Note: $0

143 GLOBAL WARMING
Referred to External Matters Committee

In an effort to preserve environmental quality, the United States government will cooperate with other governments in the world to reduce global warming. In the United States, fossil fuel use will be reduced by 5 percent beginning two years from enactment of this legislation. Alternate energy sources will be utilized to replace declining fossil fuel use. Individuals who lose their livelihoods as a result of reduction in fossil fuel use will be eligible for unemployment benefits until they find a position that will compensate them at the wage, salary and benefit level that they earned in their past occupation.

Fiscal Note: $12.5 Billion annual expenditure

144 NATIONAL REGISTRY OF CHILD MOLESTERS
Referred to Internal Matters Committee

In order to provide greater protection to children, the United States Department of Justice will create a National Registry of Child Molesters who have been tried and found guilty of child sex offenses within the borders of the United States. This registry will be available on the Internet and will include the names, current address, photo, and criminal records of convicted child molesters. Any citizen may be able to enter the name of a community and find the information about convicted molesters who live in that community. Convicted molesters are legally bound to furnish accurate information about their current addresses. Failure to furnish accurate residential information will result in a fine not to exceed one year in prison or $5,000 for each violation.

Fiscal Note: $20 Million annual expenditure

145 UNIFORM LEGAL AGE
Referred to Government Operations Committee

In an effort to promote consistency, age 18 will be the uniform age of adulthood. This age will be used to qualify for voting, military service, criminal prosecution as an adult, automotive transportation license, use of legal substances and any other adult privileges. No state may pass legislation that establishes differential treatment for a person who has attained the age of eighteen.

Fiscal Note: $0

146 MODIFICATION OF THE WAR POWERS ACT
Referred to External Matters Committee

In order to promote wider involvement by Congress in military decisions, the President will be limited to a 30-day period, rather than a 60-day period, in which troops can be sent into a hostile situation without consent of both houses of Congress. Under this modification, the President must gain approval of the House and Senate if American troops are to be put into a dangerous or potentially dangerous situation for more than 30 days.

Fiscal Note: $0

147 ADOPTION RIGHTS FOR SAME SEX COUPLES
Referred to Internal Matters Committee

In order to respect lifestyle differences and protect personal freedoms, no state may prohibit a couple of the same gender from adopting and raising a child. The sexual orientation of the adopting couple will not constitute a basis on which to grant adoption. The same sex couple may be denied adoption rights for reasons not associated with sexual orientation.

Fiscal Note: $0

148 MEDITATION IN SCHOOLS
Referred to Government Operations Committee

In order to promote moral development, any school that receives financial aid from the national government will set aside one minute each day for students to engage in silent meditation.

Fiscal Note: $0

149 ROBOTIC LAND PERSONNEL
Referred to External Matters Committee

In order to promote military readiness, the Department of Defense is authorized to develop and deploy robotic soldiers that can take the place of human soldiers in dangerous combat situations. The robotic soldiers will be able to operate weapons, be protected by bullet-deflecting shields and be able to move over land and water, as well as fly short distances with the aid of propulsion devices. The robotic soldiers will be able to be controlled from remote locations or can act independently, based on programmed information. The robotic soldiers will also have voice recognition capability allowing them to recognize and translate foreign speech into English.

This research and development will be complete within five years and will result in 500 robotic soldiers.

Fiscal Note: $ 100 Billion annual expenditure for five years

150 MANDATORY BLOOD DONATIONS
Referred to Internal Matters Committee

In an effort to increase the nation's blood supply, all drivers in states that receive federal aid for road construction will be required to make a blood donation in the year and month that their driver's license comes up for renewal. All mandatory blood donations will be made at regular Red Cross donation sites and the Red Cross will confirm donations to the automobile licensing department of the state government. Individuals who have a signed medical excuse will be exempt from this requirement.

Those who have not made their blood donations are not eligible to receive a driver's license.

Fiscal Note: $ 25 Million annual expenditure

151 FEDERAL PROSECUTORS
Referred to Government Operations Committee

In an effort to guarantee that justice will be impartial, the position of United States Attorney for each state will be changed from a position that is appointed by the President, with the appointee selected from within the President's political party. Instead, these will be civil service positions within the Department of Justice. Federal prosecutors may not be involved in the activities of any political party while employed by the Department of Justice.

Fiscal Note: $0

152 EXPANSION OF TERRITORIAL LIMITS
Referred to External Matters Committee

In an effort to increase national security, the territorial limits of the United States shall extend to 300 miles into the Atlantic and Pacific Oceans except in those cases where foreign territories might fall within this secure area. In such cases, United States territory will extend 50% of the distance into the foreign territory.

Any foreign nation must gain permission before entering into the territory of the United States for any purpose. Unauthorized travel on or beneath the seas within U.S. territory will be considered a provocative act.

Fiscal Note: $0

153 GUN SAFETY LOCKS AND WEAPON EXCHANGE
Referred to Internal Matters Committee

Out of the need to protect public safety, gun manufacturers must add an electronic lock that can only be released from a remote controlling device as well as a central controlling device. The remote-controlling device can be located near the weapon and the central controlling device will be located at the Bureau of Alcohol, Firearms and Tobacco. Such new weapons will use ammunition that will not work with conventional weapons. Ownership of older weapons will be illegal and will be purchased by the manufacturer at fair market value. These older weapons will be destroyed.

Fiscal Note: $0

154 NATIONAL CASINOS
Referred to Government Operations Committee

In order to increase revenue for national programs, the national government may establish up to eight national casinos in the continental United States. The Treasury Department will select the exact location of each casino operation.

These casinos will be leased to private companies, and a 50 percent portion of the revenue will be used to offset governmental expenditures.

Fiscal Note: $3 Billion annual revenue

155 EXPANSION OF CENTRAL INTELLIGENCE AGENCY AUTHORITY
Referred to External Matters Committee

In order to increase American flexibility to foreign threats, the Central Intelligence Agency is authorized to engage in direct assassination efforts to remove foreign government leaders who are detrimental to the national interest of the United States. In order to plan and implement an assassination effort using Central Intelligence Agency operatives, the CIA must receive permission of the President and all other means must be exhausted.

Fiscal Note: $3 million annual expenditure

156 MULTI-LINGUAL EDUCATION
Referred to Internal Matters Committee

In order to keep America competitive in the global economy and adapt to increasing cultural diversity within the United States, the national government will assist local school districts in requiring that graduates be familiar with two other languages in addition to their native languages. School districts that participate will receive grants of $100,000 for every 1,000 students in order to hire full- and part-time language instructors. Such instruction will begin in the primary grades and will be available throughout a student's education.

Fiscal Note: $15 Billion annual expenditure

157 INSANITY DEFENSE
Referred to Government Operations Committee

In an effort to promote a responsible justice system, the insanity defense will no longer be possible in federal criminal cases. Individuals may no longer claim that they were not responsible for their actions, either permanently or temporarily, due to their state of mind. Once in prison, a convicted criminal may seek psychological counseling.

Fiscal Note: $0

158 NORMAL TRADING RELATIONSHIPS
Referred to External Matters Committee

In order to regularize trade patterns, trading relationships with other nations will be determined by the President. All nations will automatically be regarded as having normal trading relationships with the United States unless the President determines that specific internal or external policies of particular foreign governments are repugnant to American values. In those cases, American businesses are not permitted to export or import goods or services or to engage in any economic transactions with organizations within that country.

Fiscal Note: $0

159 PLANT-CLOSING AND COMMUNITY IMPACT
Referred to Internal Matters Committee

In an effort to help communities adapt to the loss of a major employer, any company that engages in interstate commerce and plans to close a local manufacturing, distribution or other type of facility, must give a five-year notice of its intentions. Moreover, the company must establish a plant-closing fund to continue the wages, salaries and benefits of workers six months after the final closing of a facility. Workers who have been offered their old position in a new state or community will not be eligible to receive support from the plant-closing fund.

Fiscal Note: $0

160 CONGRESSIONAL TERM LIMITS
Referred to Government Operations Committee

In order to promote a government that is more responsive to citizen needs and desires, no member of the House of Representatives or the United States Senate may serve more than two consecutive terms of office. This will go into effect with the next election, and any currently elected member of Congress will not be affected.

Fiscal Note: $0

161 STRATEGIC USE OF FOREIGN CURRENCIES
Referred to External Matters Committee

In order to increase the number of options that the United States has in its relationships with other nations, the national government creates a Strategic Currency Reserve Fund. This fund is authorized to slowly buy, and then quickly sell, large sums of specific foreign currencies. These actions would be taken in an effort to destabilize political systems that are threats or unfriendly to American interests.

Assets of this fund will be managed by the Department of Defense in order to increase ownership of foreign currency reserves. The President must authorize any strategic sale that would have a negative effect on a foreign political system.

Fiscal Note: $ 30 Billion annual expenditure

162 MANDATORY SIGNALING DEVICE
Referred to Internal Matters Committee

In order to promote safety and reduce the number of highway accidents, all new-model motorized vehicles will have automatic signaling devices installed as standard equipment. These devices will detect that the vehicle driver has turned the wheel 15 degrees or more in either direction. This change will automatically activate the appropriate turn signal and alert other drivers that a vehicle is changing directions.

Fiscal Note: $0

163 PERSONAL AND CORPORATE CREDIT LIMITS
Referred to Government Operations Committee

In order to promote economic growth and stability, the Federal Reserve Board is authorized to raise and lower maximum borrowing limits for corporations and individuals.

The Federal Reserve Board will establish an inventory of credit ratings and maximum credit limits for all borrowers. The Board may then raise or lower credit limits for all or some borrowers in order to stimulate or slow down spending in the economy.

This new authority of the Federal Reserve Board will supplement its existing capacity to raise and lower interest rates in the economy.

Fiscal Note: $ 250 Million annual expenditure

164 INTERNATIONAL MONETARY STABILIZATION
Referred to External Matters Committee

In order to promote economic growth based on sound economic decisions, the United States may no longer buy a foreign currency to stabilize the price of that currency when a foreign economy is undergoing economic difficulties. In the absence of American stabilization efforts, currency values will more likely be determined by supply and demand.

Fiscal Note: $1 Billion annual savings

165 PHYSICIAN ASSISTED SUICIDE
Referred to Internal Matters Committee

In order to promote more humane medical practice, no medical doctor may be prosecuted for taking the life of another person in the event that the life was taken to end the patient's pain and suffering. In order for a licensed physician to terminate the life of any person, the patient or the patient's representative, plus three other physicians, must agree in writing that there is sufficient cause.

Fiscal Note: $0

166 PROHIBIT USE OF CAPITAL PUNISHMENT
Referred to Government Operations Committee

Out of respect for human life, the national government prohibits the use of capital punishment for even the most serious crimes. No government within the United States has the right to take a life. Moreover, capital punishment constitutes a type of "cruel and unusual punishment" that is prohibited by the Eighth Amendment to the United States Constitution.

Fiscal Note: $ 3 Million annual expenditure for life sentences

167 REFUGEES
Referred to External Matters Committee

In order to restrict immigration into this country, the United States will no longer accept political refugees from other political systems. These refugees, who seek asylum because of political persecution in their home countries, will not be able to legally enter the United States or become citizens. Such refugees are the responsibility of their home country, or of other nations who agree to accept these persons.

Fiscal Note: $5 Million annual savings

168 ELIMINATION OF PERSONAL OR CORPORATE BANKRUPTCY
Referred to Internal Matters Committee

In an effort to promote greater responsibility for personal economic decisions, existing law will be modified to eliminate bankruptcy as an option for individuals and corporations. Courts may lengthen the period of time in which individuals and corporations must pay their debts. However, creditors must be paid and debtors will not be able to avoid their obligations.

Fiscal Note: $0

169 DISTRICT OF COLUMBIA STATEHOOD AMENDMENT
Referred to Government Operations Committee
Two-thirds approval of each House needed

The Twenty Third Amendment to the United States Constitution is hereby repealed.

The District constituting the seat of the national government will become a state government. It shall form its own legislative, executive and judicial branches and shall elect two Senators and as many Representatives in Congress as its population justifies. The District of Columbia shall also have a number of electoral votes equal to the number of Senators and Representatives from the new state.

Fiscal Note: $700 Million annual expenditure

170 EXECUTIVE AGREEMENTS
Referred to External Matters Committee

In order to create wider involvement in critical foreign policy decisions, the President of the United States will no longer be able to make executive agreements with other nations that would be binding on future U.S. administrations without the consent of Congress. In the future, all such agreements would be submitted to U.S. Senate for approval.

Fiscal Note: $0

171 ALCOHOL LITIGATION FUND
Referred to Internal Matters Committee

In order to redress problems associated with alcohol consumption, companies that manufacture alcoholic beverages for sale within the United States are obligated to add 20 percent to the cost of the product to support an Alcohol Litigation Fund. This fund will be used to make financial awards for lawsuits from former alcohol drinkers who have died or suffered from the effects of drinking, and those whose health may have been damaged by others' use of alcohol. No suits outside of this fund are allowable.

Fiscal Note: $0

172 HOME OWNERSHIP INCENTIVE
Referred to Government Operations Committee

In order to provide for community stability, homeowners will be able to deduct 125 percent of their mortgage interest and property tax expenses from the federal income tax. In order to benefit from this provision, the homeowner must have owned the property for at least a year, and it must be the owner's principal place of residence.

Fiscal Note: $3 Billion lost annual revenue

173 EXPANSION OF NORTH AMERICAN FREE TRADE AGREEMENT
Referred to External Matters Committee

In order to promote economic progress in North America, the United States proposes an amendment of the North American Free Trade agreement that would allow for the inclusion of new free trade partner nations from Central America. These new nations would have the same rights under the treaty as Canada, Mexico and the United States.

Fiscal Note: $0

174 LONG TERM CARE
Referred to Internal Matters Committee

In order to protect citizens against the high costs of illness or injury requiring long term care, the United States establishes a Long Term Care Fund that would pay long term care insurance premiums for every American. This fund would be supported by a 1 percent tax on all goods and services that move between states. Consumers would be able to select their own insurance company.

Fiscal Note: $20 Billion annual expenditure and revenue

175 BAN ON LABOR UNION STRIKES, BINDING ARBITRATION
Referred to Government Operations Committee

In an effort to minimize disruption of the American economy, labor unions will no longer be able to strike for higher wages or changes in working conditions. Unions may represent workers and negotiate with management. In situations in which unions and management cannot agree, neutral arbitrators will be used, and the results will be binding on both sides.

Fiscal Note: $1 Million annual expenditure

176 IMPROVEMENTS TO MILITARY RETIREMENTS
Referred to External Matters Committee

In an effort to compensate those who have risked their lives in defense of their country, all retired military personnel will receive a 10 percent increase in their annual retirement payments. Such an increase will be built into future costs of military retirements.

Fiscal Note: $600 Million annual expenditure

177 SPORTS FRANCHISES
Referred to Internal Matters Committee

In order to provide greater predictability in the sports entertainment industry, the national government mandates that sports franchises will be able to be bought and sold on the open market. However, these franchises cannot move. If owners close down a franchise, those owners may not participate in any other sports franchise, in that sport or any other professional sport.

Fiscal Note: $0

178 SUPREME COURT TERMS AMENDMENT
Referred to Government Operations Committee
Two-thirds approval of each House needed

Supreme Court terms will no longer be held indefinitely.

The President will appoint justices to the Supreme Court for ten-year terms with the consent of the Senate as vacancies occur. Justices may succeed themselves in office if re-appointed. The Chief Justice will be elected by the justices of the Supreme Court, and will serve a five-year term.

Fiscal Note: $0

179 DECLARATION OF WAR
Referred to External Matters Committee

In order to create more legislative involvement in critical military decisions, a Declaration of War will be necessary in any situation in which American military personnel may be involved in combat. The President may no longer send the U.S. military into action without a full Declaration of War.

Fiscal Note: $0

180 NARCOTIC SUBSTANCES
Referred to Internal Matters Committee

In order to promote greater consistency with regard to narcotics, the United States will have a uniform policy on narcotic substances. The Food and Drug Administration may regulate and tax the importation, exportation, manufacture and sale of all addictive and non-addictive narcotic substances.

Fiscal Note: $5 Billion annual revenue

181 BALANCED BUDGET AMENDMENT
Referred to Government Operations Committee
Two-thirds approval of each House needed

The national government budget will be balanced on an annual basis. Total expenditures may not exceed total revenues in any year. Surpluses may be carried over from year to year to meet unexpected emergencies.

Fiscal Note: $0

182 PRIVATIZATION OF WORLD BANK
Referred to External Matters Committee

In order to promote economic efficiency, the U.S. will continue to loan money to the World Bank for assistance to less-developed nations throughout the world as long as the World Bank creates economic incentives for the recipient nations. Continued U.S. involvement will be premised on the assurance that the World Bank will apply the principles of private enterprise, and distribute profits to contributing nations. Such profits will be obtained by being more restrictive in loans and by increasing interest rates to nations that borrow from the World Bank.

Fiscal Note: $100 million annual revenue

183 COMMUNITY RENEWAL
Referred to Internal Matters Committee

In an effort to revitalize older neighborhoods and slow down the process of suburban sprawl, the United States will invest in older communities. Communities that are 50 years or older will be eligible for federal funds to improve streets, roads and sidewalks, as well as public buildings. In addition, property owners in these communities will be able to subtract the cost of repairs and improvements from the amount of federal income taxes owed.

More recently constructed communities will not be eligible for these funds.

Fiscal Note: $27 Billion dollar annual revenue decline

184 TWO-WAY TELEVISIONS
Referred to Government Operations Committee

In an effort to gather evidence in criminal cases, all new televisions will contain a camera and microphone that can be used to observe individuals who might be engaged in illegal activities.

A court order will be necessary for the camera and/or microphone to be activated. Any evidence gathered by the camera and/or microphone without a court order will be not be admitted in judicial proceedings. Use of two-way television for civil cases is strictly prohibited.

Fiscal Note: $0

185 RELIGIOUS GROUPS AND THE MILITARY
Referred to External Matters Committee

In order to promote religious freedom, the United States military will provide free and open access to all religious groups that seek to minister to members of their religion within the military, as well as allow religious groups to recruit converts from within the armed services. Any costs incurred will be the responsibility of the religious groups involved, and activities of religious groups will be allowed as long as they do not interfere with combat requirements of military personnel.

Fiscal Note: $0

186 PRESCRIPTION DRUG COST
Referred to Internal Matters Committee

In order to reduce the cost of prescription drugs for consumers, the national government will reduce the time necessary to gain approval for the manufacture of a new drug, and the national government will underwrite part of the costs of new drug research. The time for approval of new drugs will be reduced to 30 days from the date of application if preliminary evidence shows the medical benefits of the new drug. In addition, the national government will provide funds for new drug research and thus lower the overall cost of such research.

Fiscal Note: $5.5 Billion annual expenditure

187 CONGRESSIONAL DISTRICT BOUNDARIES
Referred to Government Operations Committee

In an effort to ensure that the districts of members of the United States House of Representatives are equal in population size and compact in shape, the Federal Elections Commission will realign districts after every national census. No district can be more than 5 percent larger or smaller than the average district. The six-member, bipartisan commission will present the new design for districts at a minimum of one year prior to a congressional election.

Fiscal Note: $10 Million annual expenditure

188 USE OF MERCENARIES
Referred to External Matters Committee

In an effort to bolster national security, the United States will supplement its normal military operations with funds to support mercenary military personnel who do not have loyalties to any particular nation. These mercenaries will be deployed to achieve limited goals in situations when the President wishes to achieve a military objective without risking the loss of lives or injury among American military personnel.

Fiscal Note: $ 2.5 Billion annual expenditure

189 FAMILY PROGRAMMING ON TELEVISION
Referred to Internal Matters Committee

In an effort to counteract the impact of violent and sexually oriented programs on television, every television channel will dedicate at least 20 percent of its time to family oriented programming. This programming will be offered between 2:00 p.m. and midnight.

Fiscal Note: $0

190 LOYALTY OATHS FOR TEACHERS
Referred to Government Operations Committee

All current and future teachers in K-12 schools as well as universities and colleges in schools that receive federal aid will sign a loyalty oath as a condition of employment.

The loyalty oath will read as follows: "I hereby swear my allegiance to the United States and will not promote the interests of any other nation or international group. In pursuit of this, I will not subvert the United States in the classroom or in the community." Those who are not American citizens are not required to sign this oath. However, they may do so if they wish.

Fiscal Note: $ 10 Million annual expenditure

191 BAN ON FIRST STRIKE NUCLEAR WEAPONS
Referred to External Matters Committee

In the interest of world peace, the United States declares that it will not use nuclear weapons for first strike offensive purpose. The U.S. nuclear arsenal will only be used in response to an attack from a potential aggressor. This ban on first strike use of nuclear weapons does not imply reductions in the U.S. stockpile, or an unwillingness to make effective deployment of such weaponry.

Fiscal Note: $ 0

192 PHONICS LANGUAGE TEACHING
Referred to Internal Matters Committee

In order to improve the quality of education for elementary and secondary students, the national government will supply financial assistance for participating school districts to develop and teach reading units based on the phonics method. Other methods may also be used to build on the phonics skill foundation. Participating schools will be eligible for a per student share of total annual funding.

Fiscal Note: $6.5 Billion annual expenditure

193 FAST FOOD TRASH TAX
Referred to Government Operations Committee

In order to protect our environment from discarded trash associated with fast food consumption, the national government establishes a 2% tax on all fast food purchases. Revenue will be redistributed to the states, according to state population size, and may only be used for (1) removing trash from streets, roads, curbs, sidewalks and water supply; (2) recycling, plus (3) public information campaigns.

Fiscal Note: $2.2 Billion annual revenue

194 EXPANSION OF NATO
Referred to External Matters Committee

In order to promote international peace, the United States urges the expansion of the North Atlantic Treaty Organization. This expansion would include additional member nations from other parts of the world that have records of being peaceful nations. Such new members would seek to strengthen the security goals of NATO and would be able to receive support from all NATO partners if attacked by a hostile power. The U.S. urges that any nation applying for membership in NATO receive unanimous support from all current NATO member nations.

The expanded NATO will not only serve as a mutual defense organization. It will also serve as an organization to produce stability in world politics.

Fiscal Note: $ 0

195 WORKWEEK LENGTH
Referred to Internal Matters Committee

Out of the desire to increase productivity during work hours and increase new employment opportunities, the national government will mandate a 30-hour working week for all salaried and hourly workers in the United States. Total compensation for individual employees will not be reduced in this modification of the workweek. This legislation will not apply to workers employed in agriculture.

Fiscal Note: $0

196 NATIONAL SERVICE
Referred to Government Operations Committee

In an effort to encourage all citizens to become involved in public service and accomplish needed projects, a National Service Program will be established, and participation in this program will be mandatory for all students graduating from high school or attaining age 18. Those enlisting in the military will be exempt from the National Service Program.

Individuals will be paid a minimal wage and have health care benefits during their two years of service. At the conclusion of National Service, an individual will receive a grant not to exceed $10,000 per year for four years to attend any undergraduate institution in which they gain acceptance. Individuals will continue to receive their grants as long as they are taking normal loads and have 3.0 grade point averages.

Fiscal Note: $8 Billion annual expenditure

197 AVOIDANCE OF MILITARY OPERATIONS ON CIVILIAN TARGETS
Referred to External Matters Committee

In an effort to differentiate between foreign government threats and civilian populations of those countries, the United States will avoid attacks on civilian targets in situations where U.S. forces are involved in combat. Housing, heath care, educational and religious facilities will not be targets. Attacks will be directed at military targets and those political and industrial facilities that support the military readiness of a hostile nation.

Fiscal Note: $ 0

198 LAND FILL MANAGEMENT
Referred to Internal Matters Committee

In order to cope with rising amounts of solid waste, the national government will purchase landfill sites throughout the United States in locations throughout the 50 states. The sites in each state will have a total capacity that will accommodate all of the solid waste that is discarded from that particular state.

Fiscal Note: $7 Billion annual expenditure

199 NATIONAL VEHICLE TAX
Referred to Government Operations Committee

In an effort to encourage energy conservation, the national government will levy a tax on all new automobiles based on fuel efficiency. Sellers may calculate the tax by adding city and highway mileage figures for the vehicle being sold, and subtracting this amount from $300. The remaining amount will be paid to the national government.

Fiscal Note: $15 Billion annual revenue

200 IMPORTATION OF GENETIC MATERIAL FROM ABORTED FETUSES
Referred to External Matters Committee

In an effort to promote health, medical organizations may import genetic material from aborted fetuses for positive medical applications. Those in the foreign nations selling the aborted fetuses must assure the purchaser that the abortions were medically necessary. Moreover, purchasers must use the genetic material to improve the health of American citizens.

Fiscal Note: $0

201 ELECTIVE MEDICAL PROCEDURES
Referred to Internal Matters Committee

In an effort to meet the medical needs of patients, insurance companies will now cover elective procedures as long as a physician recommends these procedures. Physicians may recommend procedures if they believe that the procedures will improve the overall health or well being of the patient. No insurance company may disallow payment for elective surgical procedures.

Fiscal Note: $0

202 REPRODUCTIVE RIGHTS
Referred to Government Operations Committee

In order to protect personal freedom, no state government shall restrict an individual's right to obtain information about reproduction, as well as methods of preventing reproduction. Moreover, no state may prohibit abortions during the first trimester of pregnancy.

It will be a federal crime for anyone to harass an individual who is exercising reproductive rights. This crime is punishable by a fine of $25,000 per violation.

Fiscal Note: $0

203 RENUNCIATION OF WAR AMENDMENT TO THE U.S. CONSTITUTION
Referred to External Matters Committee
Two-thirds approval of each House needed

The United States renounces the use of war to achieve national political objectives, and, in addition, will reduce U.S. military forces to a level that can only support domestic security activities. Furthermore, the United States vows to achieve its international political objectives through non-military means.

Fiscal Note: $260 Billion in annual savings

204 LICENSING OF GUN BUYERS
Referred to Internal Matters Committee

In order to promote public safety, the Bureau of Alcohol, Tobacco and Firearms will issue licenses to gun purchasers. Licenses will only be issued after a 90-day background investigation to determine if the applicant has a criminal record or is regarded as mentally unstable. Every applicant will undergo a psychological evaluation to determine his or her fitness to be a gun owner.

Fiscal Note: $1 Billion annual expenditure

205 STATES RIGHTS CONSTITUTIONAL AMENDMENT
Referred to Government Operations Committee
Two-thirds approval of each House needed

Those responsibilities reserved to the states in the Tenth Amendment to the United States Constitution will, in all cases, be superior to the laws and treaties of the national government. Any state's laws and regulations will take precedence over national legislation, regulation or international agreements.

Fiscal Note: $0

206 ANTI-TERRORISM ACT
Referred to External Matters Committee

In order to protect the vital interests of the United States, the national government will use all of its intelligence-gathering and military capabilities to wage permanent war on perpetrators and supporters of international terrorism. National government personnel are authorized to take whatever action is necessary to eliminate acts of terrorism and these actions may take place within the United States or in other countries.

Fiscal Note: $2.5 Billion annual expenditure

207 DRUG ABUSE
Referred to Internal Matters Committee

In order to combat drug trafficking and drug abuse within the United States, the national government authorizes federal agents to infiltrate drug trafficking organizations and plant drugs that contain toxic substances. The purpose of these actions is to substantially increase the risk of taking drugs and to make traffickers less reliable sources for drugs.

Fiscal Note: $3 Billion annual expenditure

208 NATIONAL LOTTERY
Referred to Government Operations Committee

In an effort to obtain needed funding, The Department of Treasury is authorized to organize a weekly national lottery to produce new revenue. Five-dollar ticket amounts, not to exceed $25 per player, may be voluntarily withheld from an individual's paycheck.

This lottery will pay out sums not to exceed $30 million each week. A $20 million grand prize and 100 secondary prizes ($100,000 per prize) will be awarded each week. All winnings will be exempt from the federal income tax.

Fiscal Note: $40 Billion in annual revenue; $1.6 Billion annual expense

209 RESTRICTION ON CIA INVOLVEMENT IN INDUSTRIAL SPYING
Referred to External Matters Committee

In order to maintain the focus of American intelligence gathering efforts, the Central Intelligence Agency may not use its personnel or other resources to obtain information from foreign companies and transfer that information to U.S. companies, thus giving American companies a competitive advantage in world markets. The Agency will dedicate its resources only to protect the political interests of the United States and to protect national security.

Fiscal Note: $0

210 FAMILY DEVELOPMENT CENTERS
Referred to Internal Matters Committee

In order to promote a positive environment for children, the national government will establish family development centers in each community in the United States. These centers will be staffed by volunteers and use space and supplies furnished by the Department of Health and Human Services. Local centers will have regular hours when families can seek help in adjusting to normal problems, as well as to get referrals for more specific services in the event of a family crisis.

Fiscal Note: $4 Billion annual expenditure

211 ENGLISH AS THE NATIONAL LANGUAGE
Referred to Government Operations Committee

In order to provide stability and raise the level of communication, English will be the official language of the United States. All legal documents will only be published in English, and all voting will be in English.

Other languages may be used for unofficial purposes.

Fiscal Note: $0

212 RECOGNITION OF CUBA
Referred to External Matters Committee

In order to promote regional peace in the Americas, the United States Government will work towards the establishment of normal diplomatic relationships with Cuba. Past differences with Cuba should be set aside in favor of a new positive relationship between the United States and the Cuban government. The United States will begin the process of normalization through exchanges and joint ventures.

Fiscal Note: $2 million annual expenditure

213 MANDATORY VEHICLE SPEED BROADCASTER
Referred to Internal Matters Committee

In an effort to reduce automobile speeds and save lives, the national government will require automobile manufacturers to install vehicle speed broadcasting devices in all new vehicles. These devices will identify a vehicle and indicate the speed of a vehicle to state and local police departments within a 25-mile range over existing police channels. Police officials will record the location, speed, date and time of any infraction and may issue speeding tickets in those cases in which the vehicle exceeds the speed limit.

States may mandate that owners of older vehicles be required to install vehicle speed broadcasting systems. The national government will provide grants of $50- $75 million to any state that imposes such requirements, depending on the number of drivers within the states.

Fiscal Note: $ 3 Billion annual expenditure

214 PRESIDENTIAL TERM CONSTITUTIONAL AMENDMENT
Referred to Government Operations Committee
Two-thirds approval of each House needed

The President will be elected for a six-year term and may serve no longer than twelve years. Any Vice President who becomes President due the death or disability of his or her predecessor may serve longer than twelve years.

This amendment will go into effect after the next Presidential election.

Fiscal Note: $0

215 ASSISTANCE TO FOREIGN SPACE PROGRAMS
Referred to External Matters Committee

In order to increase space exploration and world technological development, the United States lends support to certain foreign space programs. These programs must show a record of advancement and a willingness to share data with the American space program. The President would designate such programs.

Fiscal Note: $13 Billion annual expenditure

216 ACCOMODATIONS FOR DISABLED
Referred to Internal Matters Committee

In order to encourage accommodations for the disabled, the national government will allow businesses to directly reduce their taxes by the amount that they spend to create accommodations for the disabled. Such accommodations would apply to both customers and employees.

Fiscal Note: $7.2 Billion loss of annual revenue

217 INDEPENDENT COMPENSATION COMMISSION
Referred to Government Operations Committee

In order to establish fair compensation for government service, all salaries of Senators, United States Representatives, federal judges, as well as the President and Vice President will be set by an Independent Compensation Commission. Congress will no longer be directly involved in establishing compensation for itself or other offices.
This Commission will have six members and will equally represent major political parties. Those nominated will serve staggered 15-year terms and will be appointed by the President with the approval of the both Houses of Congress. Commission members may not succeed themselves in office.

Fiscal Note: $2 Million annual expenditure

218 DUAL CITIZENSHIP
Referred to External Matters Committee

In order to clarify the meaning of American citizenship, the concept of dual citizenship will not be recognized. If an individual claims that they have the rights of citizenship in any other country, then, any claims of American citizenship will be denied.

Fiscal Note: $ 0 annual expenditure

219 INCENTIVES FOR ACADEMIC ACHIEVEMENT
Referred to Internal Matters Committee

In an effort to promote the quality of education, the national government will create an Educational Incentive Fund that would pay monthly stipends to every elementary and secondary student above age eight. The amount of the stipend would be determined by the student's academic record. The Department of Education will establish the formula for relating grades to stipend amount.

Fiscal Note: $12 Billion annual expenditure

220 NON-PRESCRIPTION ANTI-CONCEPTION PROCEDURE
Referred to Government Operations Committee

In an effort to promote safety in coping with unwanted pregnancies, the Food and Drug Administration is authorized to approve a non-prescription electronic procedure that can be administered within 24 hours after possible conception. The Food and Drug Administration must be satisfied that the procedure is safe before it may be offered to the public.

Fiscal Note: $0

221 DEBT FORGIVENESS FOR FOREIGN NATIONS
Referred to External Matters Committee

Out of the recognition that the debtor nations have virtually no chance of paying back their loans, and that interest-only payments remove valuable funds for economic growth, the United States declares that it will forgive the debts of all the underdeveloped nations that have made good faith efforts. The U.S. government will pay back U.S. lending banks for loans made to these debtor nations over a 10-year period.

Fiscal Note: $27 Billion expenditure for 10 years

222 REGULATION OF NON-PRESCRIPTION DRUGS
Referred to Internal Matters Committee

In order to protect public health and guard against medical fraud, The Food and Drug Administration is authorized to certify that non-prescription drugs are safe if used in recommended doses, and that the advertised medical benefits are substantiated by data. New non-prescription drugs and supplements must go through a one-year review before being certified. Existing non-prescription drugs or supplements must go through a six-month review process.

Fiscal Note: $1 Billion annual expenditure

223 CONSTITUTIONAL AMENDMENT PROCEDURES
Referred to Government Operations Committee
Two-thirds approval of each House needed

A vote of 60 percent in each house will be necessary to propose an amendment, and the proposed amendment must be adopted by more than two-thirds of the states.

Fiscal Note $0

224 INTERNATIONAL SPACE STATION
Referred to External Matters Committee

In order to expedite the process of space exploration and increase international cooperation, the United States joins England, France, Russia and Japan in the creation and deployment of a new international space station. This space station, with an international crew, would be placed in an orbit around the furthest edge of the solar system. The new space station would gather data and serve as an outpost for further space exploration.

Fiscal Note: $15 Billion annual expenditure

225 MANDATORY SEAT BELTS IN BUSES
Referred to Internal Matters Committee

In an effort to promote public safety, all existing and new buses will be equipped with lap and shoulder seat belts to protect passengers. The driver and passengers will be required to use these seat belts if driving on a federally funded road. States may impose fines for failure to wear the belts.

Fiscal Note: $0

226 REPEAL OF FEDERAL INCOME TAX AMENDMENT
Referred to Government Operations Committee
Two-thirds approval of each House needed

The Sixteenth Amendment to the Constitution is hereby repealed. As a result of this action, no income tax may be collected within the United States. Other sources of revenue may be used by the national government.

Fiscal Note: $830+ Billion loss of annual revenue

227 INTERNATIONAL CURRENCY
Referred to External Matters Committee

In an effort to promote economic trade and development, the United States agrees to support the creation of an international currency that could be exchanged for the U.S. dollar. The International Monetary Fund (IMF) would manage the new currency and the value would be determined by currency fluctuation within the marketplace.

Fiscal Note: $250 Million annual expenditure

228 SCHOOL SECURITY
Referred to Internal Matters Committee

In order to minimize the number of attacks in schools, the national government will provide funds to local school systems to improve security. These funds may be spent on creating a locked protective zone surrounding school buildings, as well as metal detectors at the entry points of the protective zone and within the schools. Funds may not be spent for personnel.

Fiscal Note: $7.5 Billion annual expenditure

229 NATIONAL IDENTIFICATION NUMBER
Referred to Government Operations Committee

In order to keep accurate records, an individual's social security number will be one's national identification number. This social security/national identification number will be assigned at the time of birth or at the time of application for employment, government benefits or entrance into the United States.

As part of the identification process, a sample of an individual's DNA will be labeled and linked to the national identification number of the individual, and a graphic representation of the DNA sample will be kept in a national database.

Fiscal Note: $12 Billion annual expenditure

230 BIOLOGICAL WEAPONS ERADICATION
Referred to External Matters Committee

In order to provide greater security against the threat of biological weapons, the United States dedicates resources to the elimination of such weapons. These resources will be used to identify the locations of these targets, and military forces will be dispatched to capture and destroy this weaponry. In addition, military forces will be used to capture those who are responsible for making biological weapons and bring perpetrators to trial in the United States.

Fiscal Note: $1 Billion annual expenditure

231 SOFTWARE SUPPORT
Referred to Internal Matters Committee

In order to protect the interests of consumers, all computer software vendors must continue to support a new product for a five-year period from the date of initial release. Vendors may apply a technical support fee after the first 90 days in which the software is installed. The Federal Trade Commission is authorized to establish a Software Support Division to enforce the provisions of this legislation and to judge the claims of consumers.

Fiscal Note: $250 Million annual expenditure

232 CONGRESSIONAL CAMPAIGN FINANCE
Referred to Government Operations Committee

In an effort to prevent national special interest groups from dominating Congressional elections, all funds for Congressional elections must be raised by individual sources within the Congressional District. Groups may only donate to candidates in the district where the organization's headquarters is located.

Fiscal Note: $0

233 INCREASE SIZE OF MILITARY
Referred to External Matters Committee

In an effort to enhance military preparedness, the United States will increase active and reserve military forces by 10 percent. This personnel increase will enable the military to increase its capacity to respond to threatening domestic and international situations.

Fiscal Note: $26 Billion annual expenditure

234 STATE RESPONSIBILITY FOR AIR POLLUTION
Referred to Internal Matters Committee

In order to promote public health, the national government will allow state governments to recover medical costs associated with air pollution from other states. States bringing suit must prove that individuals and industries in another state have generated excess pollution that has been carried by prevailing winds. States may only recover the direct costs associated with medical care.

Fiscal Note: $0

235 LIMITATION ON INHERITANCE
Referred to Government Operations Committee

In order to assure that individual success is based on individual achievement and that that there will be an increase in charitable contributions, the national government will limit the amount that parents may will to, or place in trust for, their children. Upon the death of the parent, each adult child who has reached the age of 21 will be limited to an inheritance not to exceed $250,000. All remaining funds will be donated to charities that are designated by the parent, or will be taken by the government through an inheritance tax.

Fiscal Note: $25 Billion annual revenue

236 WAR CRIMES AND CRIMES AGAINST HUMANITY
Referred to External Matters Committee

In order to promote international morality, war crimes and crimes against humanity that occur in foreign countries shall be considered a crime within the United States and punishable by life imprisonment with no opportunity for parole. Those who are accused of such crimes may be tried in the United States, and punishment for such crimes may be administered in the United States.

Fiscal Note: $225 Million annual expenditure

237 HIGHER EDUCATION, STUDENT COST
Referred to Internal Matters Committee

In order to increase access to higher education for all qualified students, the national government will regulate tuition and fees and establish a deferred student loan program. Under this law, total costs to students may not increase faster than the consumer price index during the previous twelve months. Student loans will be paid back at the prime rate plus one-half percent over a ten-year period, to begin two years after a student has stopped attending college. The Department of Education is authorized to deduct repayments of loans from an individual's paycheck.

Fiscal Note: $15 Billion annual expenditure

238 FEDERAL HANDGUN LICENSE
Referred to Government Operations Committee

Out of self-defense needs, individuals may obtain a federal license to carry a pistol that can only be used if the individual is attacked. Any individual seeking such a license must show that they have reason to believe that such a weapon is necessary for self-protection. Any individual seeking such a license will also need to show that they do not have a criminal record.

Fiscal Note: $10 Million annual expenditure

239 DISTRIBUTION OF DIRECT FOREIGN ASSISTANCE
Referred to External Matters Committee

In an effort to promote high international standards, all foreign aid from the United States to other nations will be awarded only if the recipient nation supports democratic political institutions and makes sustained efforts to peacefully resolve internal ethnic and racial tensions. Nations that do not comply with these provisions will not be eligible for financial assistance from the United States. This legislation will become effective two years after passage.

Fiscal Note: $3.5 Billion in annual savings

240 ANTI-MONOPOLY LEGISLATION
Referred to Internal Matters Committee

In order to protect consumers, the Federal Trade Commission will prohibit corporate mergers that allow a company to gain more than 75 percent of the market for a particular type of product or service. Individual companies that have over 75 percent of the market must sell off part of their holdings so that they will have less than 75 percent of the market.

Fiscal Note: $0

241 ELECTORAL COLLEGE REFORM CONSTITUTIONAL AMENDMENT
Referred to Government Operations Committee
Two-thirds approval of each House needed

The President and the Vice President will be elected on the basis of a national popular vote. Individual states and territories will report the results to the federal election commission. No results will be reported until all polls are closed in all jurisdictions.

Fiscal Note: $0

242 END U.S. INVOLVEMENT IN NATO
Referred to External Matters Committee

In an effort to recognize the changing realities of world politics, the United States withdraws from the North Atlantic Treaty Organization and its activities. With the collapse of the Soviet Union and the end of the Cold War, there is no further need for the North Atlantic Treaty Organization.

Fiscal Note: $2.5 Billion annual savings

243 DESALINIZATION AND WATER SHORTAGES
Referred to Internal Matters Committee

In an effort to protect agriculture and drinking water supplies, the national government will authorize the construction of desalinization plants to convert salt water into fresh water. In total, there will be three such plants on the Atlantic Coast and another three plants on the Pacific Coast. These plants will pipe water into a system that can be directed to any region that has severe water shortages. The water piping system must connect to all states in the Continental United States and will constitute 50 percent of the total cost of the project.

Fiscal Note: $38 Billion annual expenditure

244 TAX ON AMMUNITION
Referred to Government Operations Committee

In order to reduce gun violence, the national government will impose a 100 percent tax on all ammunition that is sold at the retail level. Ammunition may only be sold to individuals who have been approved to purchase a weapon. This tax will not apply to purchases by police departments or the military.

Fiscal Note: $5 Billion annual revenue

245 WITHDRAWAL FROM UNITED NATIONS
Referred to External Matters Committee

In order to promote the long-term interests of the United States, the United States withdraws from the United Nations and notifies the United Nations that it must find new headquarters within five years of the passage of this legislation. This action is taken because the United Nations has been inefficient and ineffective and has not reflected the interests of the United States.

The United States reserves the right to confiscate the present UN headquarters property in New York City and sell it for commercial purposes. The United Nations will be compensated for any loss, based on fair market value of the property.

Fiscal Note: $2 Billion annual savings

246 ACCREDITATION OF HIGHER EDUCATIONAL INSTITUTIONS
Referred to Internal Matters Committee

In order to maintain and enhance standards in higher education, all universities and colleges will gain and retain accreditation through the United States Department of Education rather than through regional accrediting associations. All higher educational institutions will be on a five-year accreditation cycle.

Fiscal Note: $25 Million annual expenditure

247 FREEDOM OF SPEECH AND RACIAL ISSUES
Referred to Government Operations Committee

In an effort to protect the rights of citizens to speak without governmental interference, the concept of hate speech will no longer be applied. Groups that genuinely believe in racial differences and the superiority of one race over another have the right to express their views and have the right to advocate elimination of inferior races. However, this protected speech does not justify violent acts against specific racial groups.

Fiscal Note: $0

248 PERMANENT UNITED NATIONS PEACEKEEPING FORCE
Referred to External Matters Committee

In an effort to create international stability, the United States will support the creation of a permanent peacekeeping force within the United Nations. This peacekeeping force can be dispatched by a unanimous vote of the UN Security Council into any country or region that needs to be stabilized.

Fiscal Note: $1.5 Billion annual expenditure

249 CLONING
Referred to Internal Matters Committee

In an effort to promote responsible development of cloning, the Department of Health and Human Services will monitor all experimentation with regard to cloning. Any attempt to clone human beings or organs from human beings will require approval by the Congress and President.

Fiscal Note: $10 Million annual expenditure

250 INDEPENDENT COUNSEL
Referred to Government Operations Committee

In order to provide constant scrutiny of government officials, an Office of Independent Counsel will become a permanent part of the Department of Justice. All of the professional and clerical staff members of this office will be civil service employees who are not active in any political party and will be free to conduct investigations as well as prosecutions of any public official at the national level. The staff will not report to the Attorney General.

Fiscal Note: $10 Million annual expenditure

251 TARIFFS AND TRADE IMBALANCE
Referred to External Matters Committee

In order to stabilize the balance of payments between the United States and other nations, the United States will establish an automatic tariff of 15 percent on the goods of any nation whenever the United States is spending more on foreign goods from a country than the American economy is earning from that country. The tariff will stay in place until the trade imbalance is equalized.

Fiscal Note: $120 Million annual revenue

252 NATIONAL K-12 CURRICULUM
Referred to Internal Matters Committee

In an effort to promote educational opportunities for all children in the United States, a national curriculum will be developed to define those basic skills and sets of knowledge that each child will learn at each grade in public schools.

This legislation will not prohibit state school systems and local educators from developing more comprehensive curriculum goals. However, these other curriculum objectives will be accomplished with state and local resources.

Private and parochial schools will be exempt from national curriculum guidelines unless they voluntarily adopt them.

Fiscal Note: $ 27 Billion annual expenditure

253 TRUST FUNDS
Referred to Government Operations Committee

In order to maintain the financial strength of the Social Security and Medicare Trust Funds, the revenues and expenditures for these items will be removed from the operating budget of the United States. The taxes that support these trust funds may not be used for any purpose other than Social Security and Medicare payments.

Fiscal Note: $600 Billion annual revenue decline.

254 INTERNATIONAL DRUG ENFORCEMENT
Referred to External Matters Committee

In order to resist the threat of drugs, the United States government hereby provides direct assistance to those nations that prevent the production or transport within or from their borders of illegal drugs that are to be sold in the United States. The Drug Enforcement Administration will disburse these funds to those nations that are demonstrating that they have dedicated their own resources to bring a halt to international drug trafficking.

This act will be in effect for a period of five years and can be renewed for another five years. The Drug Enforcement Administration will be responsible for demonstrating that this program has resulted in a decrease in illegal drugs flowing into the United States.

Fiscal Note: $2.5 Billion annual expenditure

255 CONDOM DISTRIBUTION IN SCHOOLS
Referred to Internal Matters Committee

In order to promote responsible sexual behavior, the national government will provide funds for schools to distribute condoms to students who are above age twelve. Such distribution will be integrated into the overall educational program of the school.

Such legislation will apply to any school that receives federal funds directly or indirectly. As recipients of federal funds (through vouchers, assistance and tax credits) private and parochial schools will participate in educational programs associated with condom distribution.

Fiscal Note: $2 Billion annual expenditures

256 IMMUNITY FROM LAWSUITS
Referred to Government Operations Committee

In an effort to limit responsibility of gun manufacturers in cases involving weapons, the national government will prohibit any person or organization from bringing legal action against a weapon manufacturer when the manufacturer's product has resulted in a death or injury. This limitation does not prohibit lawsuits against a weapon manufacturer for poor workmanship that results in death or injury.

Fiscal Note: $0

257 PROTECTORATE STATUS
Referred to External Matters Committee

In order to create stability and democracy in the world, the United States gives itself the option of imposing protectorate status on countries that have gone to war with the United States and have lost. The United States can use this status as an opportunity to build democratic political institutions in authoritarian or totalitarian countries, and restrict the military development of nations that have been aggressors.

Fiscal Note: $4 Billion annual expenditure if required

258 ELIMINATION OF DAYLIGHT SAVINGS TIME
Referred to Internal Matters Committee

In order to provide more stability for individual's lives, daylight savings time will be eliminated as an annual adjustment to the calendar and clocks. The whole nation will use standard time throughout the entire year.

Fiscal Note: $0

259 LOSS OF VOTING RIGHTS CONSTITUTIONAL AMENDMENT
Referred to Government Operations Committee
Two-thirds approval of both Houses needed

The right to vote will be removed for those citizens who fail to vote for five successive national elections, or who have been found guilty of a felony crime.

Individuals can regain voting rights by doing volunteer work for government, or by working in a political campaign. A total of 1040 hours of volunteering will be needed to restore voting rights, and such restoration will only be temporary. Additional failure to vote will result in automatic and permanent loss of voting rights.

Fiscal Note: $0

260 POPULATION CONTROL OF LESS DEVELOPED NATIONS
Referred to External Matters Committee

In order to reduce population growth, the United States will furnish foreign aid to those less developed nations that promote population control through contraception, birth control medication or abortions. Foreign assistance will also be furnished if these countries practice natural birth control methods to reduce birth rates.

Fiscal Note: $2.5 Billion in annual expenditure

261 GENETIC ENGINEERING
Referred to Internal Matters Committee

In an effort to provide public oversight, a Genetic Engineering Commission will be appointed by the President and confirmed by the Senate. The six-member Commission will contain scientific and religious experts. This Commission will promote and regulate agricultural and medical genetic engineering activities in the United States.

Fiscal Note: $45 Million annual expenditure

262 NATIONAL DEBT
Referred to Government Operations Committee

In an effort to build national stability for the United States, no further national debt may be incurred and the existing national debt will be paid back on a strict schedule. In order to avoid building up additional debt, each increase in spending will be matched by a tax on gasoline.

The current national debt will be paid back over a ten-year period from a tax on amusement products and services.

Fiscal Note: $600 Billion expenditure for ten years

263 IMMIGRATION QUOTAS
Referred to External Matters Committee

In an effort to reverse past immigration policies and end patterns of discrimination, the Immigration and Naturalization Service, will redesign quotas for each nation. Without increasing the total number of immigrants, increased numbers of immigrants from Asia, Africa and Latin America will be allowed and the number of immigrants from Europe will be reduced.

New quotas will be put into place two years after passage of this legislation, and will be phased in over a three-year period of time.

Fiscal Note: $0

264 EQUALIZED EDUCATIONAL EXPENDITURES
Referred to Internal Matters Committee

In order to promote equal educational opportunity in the United States, each state government will be required to equalize financial expenditures on a per student basis in public schools within that state. The national government will provide educational block grants to states to enable all states to spend at the same per student level as the most affluent state. After including federal assistance, state expenditures may not vary by more than 1 percent on a per student basis.

Fiscal Note: $35 Billion annual expenditure

265 LIABILITY FUND
Referred to Government Operations Committee

In order to minimize the number of frivolous lawsuits against businesses, the national government establishes a Liability Fund that will be used to pay claims against businesses. This fund will be managed by a five-member Liability Commission that will be appointed by the President with the consent of the Senate. Half of the annual contributions to this fund will come from a liability tax on businesses and the other half will come from general revenue.

The five-member Liability Commission will consider all the evidence regarding a claim and will make financial awards to claimants if appropriate. No further legal action will be allowed. Commission members will be appointed for seven-year staggered terms.

Fiscal Note: $5 Billion revenue and $2.5 Billion expenditure

266 WITHDRAWAL OF ASSISTANCE FOR NON-STRATEGIC COUNTRIES
Referred to External Matters Committee

In order to promote American interests, the United States will withdraw all foreign assistance from countries that are not of direct strategic value. It will no longer be acceptable to provide assistance exclusively for humanitarian reasons.

Fiscal Note: $5 Billion annual savings

267 HIGHWAY CONSTRUCTION AND IMPROVEMENT
Referred to Internal Matters Committee

In response to the increasing number of automobiles on existing highways, the national government will provide state governments with funds for new highway/road construction and maintenance.

Twenty-five percent of the contracts awarded by each state will go to minority contractors.

Fiscal Note: $40 Billion

268 ITEM VETO CONSTITUTIONAL AMENDMENT
Referred to Government Operations Committee
Two-thirds approval of each House needed

The President's veto power may extend to individual items within laws or budgets that are otherwise unacceptable to the President. Congress may strike down such a veto if two-thirds of each House of Congress so desires.

In situations of national emergency, the President may suspend the authority of Congress to negate an item veto.

Fiscal Note: $0

269 INCREASE THE RATE OF MILITARY BASE CLOSINGS
Referred to External Matters Committee

Out of the recognition that the nature of military preparedness has changed and that resources can be better used for other purposes, the United States will speed up the process of base closing. After the passage of this legislation, the military services will identify those bases that will be closed to reduce the overall number of bases, and speed up the schedule of actual base closings. All bases scheduled for closing will be deactivated within five years.

Fiscal Note: $7.5 Billion savings for five years.

270 DRIVING AGE
Referred to Internal Matters Committee

Out of the desire to help younger citizens fully participate in society, the national government permits all individuals who have reached age fifteen to obtain a driver's license. States will grant licenses if the individual is free of a criminal record and has passing grades. Applicants must also have completed a driver education course, as well as passed both a written exam and a driving exam. States may use a driving simulator for the driving test.

Fiscal Note: $0

271 UNIFORM AGE FOR ADULT CRIMES
Referred to Government Operations Committee

In order to promote public safety, an individual will be considered an adult at age 16 for federal government crimes. This action is taken because juvenile offenders are committing adult crimes and are currently free of adult sanctions. Such juvenile offenders account for a substantial portion of crime.

State governments may also lower the age for state and local criminal offenses at the individual state government's discretion.

Fiscal Note: $ 0 expenditure

272 SHARING TECHNOLOGY WITH LESS DEVELOPED COUNTRIES
Referred to External Matters Committee

In order to promote economic development in less developed nations, the United States will purchase obsolete computer technology from American companies and distribute this technology to less developed countries. The recipient countries are obligated to pay for all shipping expenses.

Fiscal Note: $3.2 Billion annual expenditure

273 MEDICAL ETHICS BOARD
Referred to Internal Matters Committee

In order to promote quality health care, a Medical Ethics Board will be established by the national government. The Board will grant approval for new medical procedures and treatments. The seven members will be appointed by the President and will be confirmed by the Senate. The members will serve six-year staggered terms.
The Board will include members from scientific backgrounds, as well as practicing physicians, academic and business leaders.

Fiscal Note: $750 Million annual expenditure

274 SEXUAL ORIENTATION AND DISCRIMINATION
Referred to Government Operations Committee

In an effort to eliminate discrimination based on sexual orientation, sexual orientation will be added to the protected classes in civil rights legislation. Any individual may bring lawsuits against any individual or organization for discrimination based on sexual orientation.

This act will go into effect one year after passage, and no discrimination lawsuits can be filed during the intervening period of time.

Fiscal Note: $0

275 RIGHTS OF CHILDREN TREATY
Referred to External Matters Committee
Ratification by Senate Required

In accordance with the proposed International Rights of Children Treaty, the United States as a signatory nation guarantees that all children in the United States government will be safe against physical and emotional abuse. No government, private organization, parent or other person may use force or intimidation against a child. A child may bring suit against any government, private organization, parent or other person who violates the rights of the child.

Fiscal Note: $0

276 AUTOMOBILE INSURANCE
Referred to Internal Matters Committee

In order to promote comprehensive insurance coverage for all drivers, a National Automobile Fund will be established from a $1 tax on each gallon of gasoline. A single insurance firm, on the basis of a competitive bid, will manage the fund for a period of two years.

Existing insurance companies may submit bids for the Fund Manager role to a newly created Automobile Insurance Commission. The Commission will be made up of seven members appointed by the President for non-consecutive terms.

The Fund Manager will pay claims and conduct investigations when it is necessary. Each July, the Fund Manager will be compensated by withdrawing 25 percent of the funds remaining after all claims have been paid.

Fiscal Note: $30 Billion in revenue and expenditure

277 NATIONAL REFERENDUM CONSTITUTIONAL AMENDMENT
Referred to Government Operations Committee
Two-thirds approval of each House needed

The Congress of the United States, with the consent of the President, may refer any pending law or Constitutional action to the voters for approval or disapproval.

Referendum elections will be held within 30 days of the congressional request for a vote.

Fiscal Note: $2 Billion annual expenditure

278 AIRLINE LANDING RIGHTS
Referred to External Matters Committee
Approval of the Senate required

In order to reduce costs and promote greater flexibility in air travel, the United States will allow foreign countries to apply for, and automatically gain, landing rights in all airports within the United States for both domestic and international flights. Such foreign airlines are still liable to pay landing taxes and other charges at local airports.

In return for this flexibility, the United States will gain unlimited access to foreign airline travel markets.

Fiscal Note: $0

279 EXPANSION OF NATIONAL FORESTS AND RECREATION AREAS
Referred to Internal Matters Committee

In order to conserve valuable national resources and to provide additional recreation activities, the Interior Department is authorized to increase the inventory of national forest land as well as land in national parks.

This new initiative will continue for 20 years. None of the new forest land may be leased to logging or mining firms. The new reserves are to be kept in a natural state and will be opened to the public after a five-year development period.

Fiscal Note: $5 Billion annual expenditure

280 CORPORATE PUBLIC SERVICE
Referred to Government Operations Committee

In an effort to encourage corporations to contribute to public services, the national government will decrease the tax liability for corporations that make charitable contributions in the form of public service. Corporations may deduct 125 percent of the cost associated with public service contributions in calculating corporate income taxes that might be due.

Corporations may not count donations to any organization that helps the corporation achieve its political interests. Corporations may also not count contributions to groups that have a history of discrimination or that advocate violence.

Provisions of this act may not be used to reduce past tax liability or be used to offset losses. It may only be used as a deduction in the year that the contribution was taken.

This act will go into effect one year after passage, and contributions during this period may not be carried over into the eligible tax year.

Fiscal Note: $15 Billion loss of annual revenue

National Budget

The Game of Politics©

Proposed Budget
(dollar figures = trillions , billions , millions)

REVENUE SOURCES

	Current	Request	House	Senate	Final
Individual Income Tax	0,966,877				
Corporate Income Tax	0,220,258				
Social Security Tax	0,818,834				
Excise Taxes	0,075,566				
Estate and Gift Taxes	0,026,121				
Customs And Duties	0,028,256				
Misc. Income	0,041,638				
Total Budget Receipts	2,177,550				

EXPENDITURE (by category)

	Current	Request	House	Senate	Final
National Defense	0,447,398				
Foreign Affairs	0,038,447				
Science, Space & Tech.	0,023,967				
Energy	0,002,121				
Natural Resources Envir.	0,031,163				
Agri-culture	0,026,020				
Commerce Housing Credit	0,006,816				
Transport	0,070,673				
Com-munity Develop.	0,019,097				
Education And Training	0,088,703				
Health	0,268,396				
(Medicare)	0,345,746				0,413,921
Income Security	0,359,535				

(Social Security)	0,544,821				0,648,992
Veterans Benefits	0,068,390				
Admin. of Justice	0,043,099				
General Gov't.	0,017,754				
(Net Interest)	0,211,076				0,253,115
Allowance	024,168				
Undistrib. Receipts	- 069,773				
Total Outlays	2,567,617				
Surplus/ Deficit	- 390,067				

Note: (Mandatory Expenditure)

Budget Comparisons

(dollar figures = trillions , billions , millions)

REVENUE SOURCES

	Year 1	Year 2	Year 3	Year 4	Current
Individual Income Tax	0,858,345	0,793,699	0,808,959	0,893,704	0,966,877
Corporate Income Tax	0,148,044	0,131,778	0,189,371	0,226,526	0,220,258
Social Security Tax	0,700,760	0,712,978	0,733,407	0,773,731	0,818,834
Excise Taxes	0,066,989	0,067,524	0,069,855	0,074,013	0,075,566
Estate and Gift Taxes	0,026,507	0,021,959	0,024,831	0,023,754	0,026,121
Customs And Duties	0,018,602	0,019,862	0,021,083	0,024,674	0,028,256
Misc. Income	0,033,926	0,034,542	0,032,565	0,036,443	0,041,638
Adjust Revenue Uncertain					
Total Budget Receipts	1,853,173	1,782,342	1,880,071	2,052,845	2,177,550

EXPENDITURE (by category $= trillions, billions, millions)

	Year 1	Year 2	Year 3	Year 4	Current
National Defense	0,348,555	0,404,920	0,455,908	0,465,871	0,447,398
Foreign Affairs	0,022,351	0,021,209	0,026,891	0,031,961	0,038,447
Science, Space & Tech.	0,020,767	0,020,873	0,023,053	0,024,021	0,023,967
Energy	0,000,475	- 000,735	- 000,166	0,001,441	0,002,121
Natural Resources Envir.	0,029,454	0,029,703	0,030,725	0,030,960	0,031,163
Agri-culture	0,021,966	0,022,497	0,015,440	0,030,504	0,026,020
Commerce Housing Credit	- 000,390	0,000,735	0,005,273	0,010,653	0,006,816
Transport	0,061,833	0,067,069	0,064,626	0,068,486	0,070,673
Com-munity Develop.	0,012,981	0,018,850	0,015,797	0,020,141	0,019,097
Education And Training	0,070,544	0,082,568	0,087,945	0,096,254	0,088,703
Health	0,196,544	0,219,576	0,240,134	0,257,532	0,268,396
(Medicare)	0,230,855	0,249,433	0,269,360	0,295,432	0,345,746
Income Security	0,312,530	0,334,432	0,332,837	0,350,918	0,359,535
(Social Security)	0,455,980	0,474,680	0,495,548	0,519,686	0,544,821

Veterans Benefits	0,050,984	0,057,022	0,059,779	0,068,161	0,068,390
Admin. of Justice	0,035,081	0,035,323	0,045,535	0,040,657	0,043,099
General Gov't.	0,016,905	0,023,071	0,021,822	0,018,855	0,017,754
(Net Interest)	0,170,949	0,153,073	0,160,245	0,177,948	0,211,076
Allowance				0,034,899	024,168
Undistrib. Receipts	- 047,392	- 054,382	- 058,537	- 064,976	- 069,773
Total Outlays	2,010,972	2,159,917	2,292,215	2,479,404	2,567,617
Surplus/ Deficit	- 157,799	- 377,575	- 412,144	- 426,559	- 390,067
Total Federal Debt	6,198,401	6,760,014	7,354,673	8,031,387	8,707,627

Note: (Mandatory Expenditure)

Gonder v. University of New Hampshire

After a year of study and debate, the University of New Hampshire in Durham, New Hampshire made the decision to become a completely smoke-free institution. This action recognized the dangers associated with second-hand smoke. In becoming a completely smoke-free institution, the university eliminated all areas on campus that were previously available for smokers, including parking lots.

Dr. Derek Gonder, Professor of Film Studies at the University, brought a federal anti-discrimination lawsuit against the institution. Gonder claimed that he had an addiction to nicotine and could not stop smoking. He pointed out that he had attempted to stop smoking several times under the direction of a physician in a clinic for nicotine addicts. However, Professor Gonder was unable to permanently change his behavior. In fact, Gonder's addiction to nicotine had actually increased since he began treatment.

According to a psychiatrist who testified at the trial, Dr. Gonder's addiction to nicotine constituted a disabling condition – that Gonder needed to smoke several times during the day and night so that he could perform his duties. The psychiatrist said that Professor Gonder would become hopelessly depressed if he was denied frequent access to a place on campus where he could smoke cigarettes.

According to Gonder's attorney, the university's removal of areas for smoking was direct discrimination against those who have this disability. Gonder's lawyer claimed that the university's decision to remove smoking areas singled out a whole class of people based on their disability and denied them what was required for their well being. According to Gonder's attorney, denial of the smoking areas was equivalent to denying wheelchair ramps to those who could not climb stairs.

The federal district court ruled against Dr. Gonder saying that he had no right to an area designated for smokers, and that nicotine addiction did not constitute a disabling condition under a careful reading of federal law. The judge also said that society had no obligation to help Gonder in his decision to continue engaging in self-destructive behavior and presenting a health danger to others. Gonder appealed the case to the U.S. Court of Appeals in Boston.

When arguing their case before the federal court of appeals, Gonder's attorneys stressed that smokers were increasingly treated as a separate and unequal group in society. They noted that organizations were establishing a new system of segregation in which smokers were the ones whose rights were being ignored. The attorneys noted that this pattern of segregation was particularly appalling to smokers who were addicted to nicotine and could not choose to stop smoking.

Attorneys for the university said that the university had every right to protect the vast majority of faculty, students and visitors from the dangers of second-hand smoke. The university also emphasized that nicotine addiction was not specifically protected under federal law.

The federal court of appeals overturned the district court and ruled that the University of New Hampshire decision was, indeed, one more step in treating smokers as a separate and unequal group in society. The court of appeals was particularly concerned with the district court's complete disregard for the disabling nature of nicotine addiction. According to the court of appeals, nicotine could be just as addictive as alcohol or other legal drugs.

The case has been appealed to and accepted by the U.S. Supreme Court.

Webster v. Board of Education of Toledo

The Board of Education of Toledo, Ohio passed a "get-tough-on-drugs" policy that authorized schools to obtain unannounced mandatory urine samples from most public school students who attend the Toledo School District. The Board had already established such a requirement for employees.

This policy grew out a drug problem that was rampant among students in the Toledo school district. A number of students were coming to school under the influence of illegal drugs, and some had even brought drugs to school, selling them to other students.

The problem reached crisis proportions when one student died as a result of drugs that were taken while at school. The student had taken the drugs in the morning and went into cardiac arrest during an afternoon physical education class.

Under the new Board policy, a middle or high school principal could require any student, during the school day, to participate in a mandatory urine test or retest. Drug Testing Associates, a reputable firm in the Toledo area, had qualified technicians monitor the urine tests. A male technician would monitor the tests for male students and a female technician would monitor the tests for female students.

Several hundred students of varying ages were tested over the course of eight months. The heaviest concentration of testing was among those between 13 and 18. Half of those students who were tested were male and the other half were female.

Mr. and Mrs. Robert Webster became incensed when their daughter, Emily, age 12, was asked to provide a urine sample at her school. The test results showed that Emily did not have any drugs in her system. However, the parents took the case to court anyway.

Attorneys for the Websters contended that the search was unconstitutional and violated Emily's privacy. The lawyers for the Websters claimed that the urine test was humiliating for Emily and created the impression that she was guilty.

The school system argued that this was a public safety issue and that students needed to be tested in order to eradicate the problem. The lawyers for the school board also argued that this was a reasonable search and there was no injury to Emily. They noted that students who were tested were chosen at random and there was absolutely no assumption of guilt.

The Websters won in the state Circuit Court in Toledo. That court held that the search was unreasonable since Emily had not displayed any suspicious behavior and the test conveyed an assumption of probable guilt. The Board of Education appealed the case to the Ohio Supreme Court.

The state Supreme Court ruled in favor of the School Board and contended that the drug problem merited a serious response. The state Supreme Court also held that the search was reasonable because the search process for each day was random, and Emily was not singled out for special treatment.

Emily's parents, with the help of the American Association for Civil Liberties, appealed to the U.S. Supreme Court. The Supreme Court has decided to hear the case.

Lapin v. Federal Communications Commission

Joel Lapin, an Arizona inventor and businessman developed a device called the *V-Chip Buster* that allowed individuals to disable the *V-Chip* and thus gain access to violent and sexually explicit material on television. Congress had passed legislation that required that the *V-Chip* be installed in televisions so parents could restrict the television viewing options of their children.

The *V-Chip Buster*, as advertised on television, sold for $19.95 and was available in convenience stores and video stores throughout the United States. Sales of the hand held *V-Chip Buster* grew, and it was a very popular item among adolescents 9-17 years of age. Concerned parents became outraged.

After the controversy developed, sales of the *V-Chip Buster* increased dramatically. At that point, Lapin launched a television campaign aimed at kids and told them that they had the right to choose what they watched on television.

The Federal Communications Commission (FCC) had the responsibility for enforcing the *V-Chip* legislation and determined that Lapin's company was in violation of the spirit of the law, ordering that all sales of the *V-Chip Buster* be discontinued.

Lapin brought suit against the FCC and contended that the original legislation did not strictly prohibit manufacturing and distributing devices to neutralize the *V-Chip*. The FCC argued that their interpretation was reasonable and that the interstate commerce clause allowed them to regulate this activity.

Lapin's lawyers countered that the *V-Chip Buster* is like a radar detector and that it is not necessarily used for improper purposes. Moreover, Lapin's lawyers contended that the regulation of radar detectors and the *V-Chip Buster* is properly a state government matter, and the national government did not have the right to regulate the sale or use of these items.

Lapin won in a federal district court in Arizona, and the court ruled that the original legislation did not provide for regulation of devices to circumvent the *V-Chip*. The district court contended that the judicial branch should not undertake to do the job of the legislature.

The FCC appealed the case to the U.S. Court of Appeals in San Francisco, arguing that society had a right to defend itself against those who would undermine our value system. The FCC emphasized that Lapin had violated the spirit of the legislation and the courts could carry out the intent of Congress. Lapin's attorneys contended that their client was operating within the law and that the FCC had overstepped its boundaries—deliberately taking on the legislative role when it decided what Congress meant, and then taking action based on that assumption.

The court of appeals ruled in favor of the FCC and held that the original law could not be implemented if the *V-Chip* could be neutralized. The court of appeals held that the new *V-Chip Buster* was open to regulation by the national government, and that it was proper for the judicial branch to carry out the intent of the Congress.

The case was then appealed to the Supreme Court. The Supreme Court has agreed to hear the case.

Dillingwoth v. California

Officer T. J. Mathis pulled Lance Dillingworth over for aggressive driving on a Los Angeles freeway. While in her police car, Officer Mathis used her computer to check Dillingworth's California driving record and discovered that he had been found guilty of three moving violations over the last year-and-a-half. At that point, Mathis issued a ticket for aggressive driving.

After going home, Officer Mathis decided to see if there were any informal reports on Dillingworth's driving on DangerousDriver.org, a new website. This website was created to give safe drivers an opportunity to give detailed reports on dangerous driving incidents, providing the license number of the vehicle and describing the driver. Before any such reports are put on the website, contributors must repeat information in writing and sign a statement expressing their willingness to verify their claims in court. This site had grown in popularity and had captured the attention of careful drivers as well as concerned parents.

When Mathis entered Dillingworth's California vanity tag number (MY ROAD) into the website's searchable database, she discovered that over the past two years there were 37 reports from other drivers of dangerous driving by a male who fit Dillingworth's description. These dangerous driving incidents included excessive speed, rapid lane changes, failing to use signals, tailgating and combinations of these behaviors.

When Dillingworth's traffic case was heard at the Los Angeles Superior Court, Officer Mathis described the aggressive driving that she witnessed and noted the information in the defendant's California driving record as well as the 37 incidents described on DangerousDriver.org. Judge Alan Lester then examined both the driving record as well as the website. After that, Judge Lester found Dillingworth guilty of aggressive driving, fined him and issued a maximum number of points on his driving record. A few days after the trial, Dillingworth's auto insurance company cancelled his policy. Moreover, no other company would issue a policy. Without insurance, Dillingworth had to quit his job as traveling salesman.

Dillingworth appealed his case to the California Court of Appeals. His lawyer argued that the traffic court judge should never have admitted evidence from the website, because such evidence was based on observations from those who were not trained to evaluate driving habits. Also, in the appeals court, Dillingworth's attorney was able to get representatives from the insurance companies to admit that they consulted the website before making the decision to deny insurance to Mr. Dillingworth. The lawyer for the State of California argued that the website was a matter of free speech and that it could be consulted by the officer, the judge and the insurance companies. Moreover, the state argued that Dillingworth's driving record speaks for itself and that the website only underscored a pattern of dangerous driving as observed by other citizens.
The California Court of Appeals reversed the decision of the traffic court judge and ordered the insurance companies to provide insurance to Dillingworth.

The state and the insurance companies appealed to the California Supreme Court. The state Supreme Court then ruled that the initial traffic court decision was correct and both the local judge and the insurance companies had the right to use the website information if that information corroborated what is in the formal driving record.

The case was then appealed to the U.S. Supreme Court and the Supreme Court has decided to issue a ruling.

Acme Beauty Cream v. Committee to Reform Television

Marian Kramer became deeply concerned about a new television program where contestants, in the hope of winning a million dollar prize, engaged in humiliating activities before a national audience. The SLIMEBALLS show was building a greater following each week as contestants took on more disgusting challenges.

Ms. Kramer had written to the producer as well as network officials and asked them to modify this program so that it would be more acceptable to a general audience. Her letters, however, were never answered. As a result, she established a new organization called the Committee to Reform Television, or CRT, and she was delighted when thousands of people joined and sent contributions to her New Jersey-based organization. Most of those who joined were concerned parents and grandparents.

After several unsuccessful attempts to convince Congress and the Federal Communications Commission to increase regulation of television programming, the leaders of the Committee to Reform Television decided to organize a boycott against those who advertised on the SLIMEBALLS television program. Rather than boycott the products of all of the advertisers, the Committee to Reform Television concentrated on just one product, Acme Beauty Cream.

Initially, the manufacturers of Acme Beauty Cream ignored the boycott and viewed it as a minor inconvenience. However, the strategy to concentrate on just one advertiser proved to be wildly successful and sales of Acme Beauty Cream plummeted. In fact, the boycott was so successful that the Acme Beauty Cream Company suffered huge financial losses. Even after the company removed their advertising for SLIMEBALLS, the sales of the beauty cream continued to decline, the company's profits fell and its stock price dropped from $50 to $1 a share.

At that point, the management of Acme Beauty Cream brought a civil suit in a federal district court in New Jersey against the Committee to Reform Television. The lawyers for Acme said that the interest group had deliberately set out to destroy the company because it was a sponsor of the SLIMEBALLS show.

Acme's lawyers alleged that the Committee to Reform Television had made the conscious decision to leave other advertisers alone, because one of CRT's major contributors was the President of Pretty Good Beauty Products, a company that produces VaVoom Beauty Cream. Acme contended that CRT had engaged in a conspiracy to obstruct interstate commerce by launching the boycott. The attorney for the Committee to Reform Television said that the group's action did not constitute a conspiracy, but was only an expression of Constitutionally guaranteed rights of free speech and assembly.

The federal district court ruled for Acme Beauty Cream and held that the substantial contributions from a competitor, and the focused nature of the boycott, went far beyond normal conceptions of free speech and assembly. The district court ruled that the interest group had done irreparable damage to the company and had interfered with the marketplace. The district court fined CRT and opened the door to damage claims from Acme.

CRT appealed the case to the U.S. Court of Appeals in Philadelphia. The circuit court overturned the district court decision and held that CRT and its donors were motivated by a political agenda, and were protected by the First Amendment. The court ruled that Acme and other companies must learn to live with the risk that they take when they place their name alongside controversial television shows.

The matter has now been appealed to the U.S. Supreme Court and the Court has agreed to make a ruling on this case.

Plunkitt v. City of Lexington

Ron L. Plunkitt (age 20) and his cousin Bobby Murdock (age 24) were arrested for breaking and entering into a warehouse in Lexington, Kentucky in order to steal electronic components for luxury automobiles. Police arrested the two individuals the next day based on the legally obtained evidence that they found in the basement of

Plunkitt's home, as well as statements from witnesses saying that Plunkitt and Murdock had been seen suspiciously hanging around the warehouse the prior evening.

Mr. Plunkitt had been living with his parents since his release from a Kentucky juvenile detention facility. Murdock began living with the Plunkitt family a few years earlier after his father had died and his mother had been taken ill. Plunkitt had dropped out of high school at age 16. Murdock had withdrawn from a special education program in Lexington after he moved in with the Plunkitt family. Over the past few years, the two young men had been earning money by distributing leaflets for a pizza delivery service to individual homes in the Lexington area.

After the two were arrested, the police questioned the two men separately. During his interrogation, Bobby Murdock admitted that he had broken into the warehouse and taken the electronic components. He also said that his cousin Ronny was involved, and that Ronny had been the leader of the robbery effort. On the basis of Murdock's confession, the state brought charges of breaking and entering, as well as theft, against both individuals.

At their trials, Murdock entered a plea of guilty and Plunkitt entered a plea of not guilty. Plunkitt informed the judge that he would represent himself. In cross-examining the prosecution witnesses, including his cousin Bobby Murdock. Plunkitt aserted that all the prosecution's witnesses were lying. He called no witnesses for the defense. At the end of his trial, Plunkitt was found guilty. During the sentencing stage, Plunkitt was ordered to serve from one to three years in prison. Murdock was placed on court-ordered probation.

Plunkitt appealed his guilty conviction because he contended that his cousin Bobby Murdock was mentally retarded, and that Bobby's confession was both coerced and untrue. Plunkitt's attorney (from a legal defense fund) obtained a psychological evaluation that demonstrated that Bobby Murdock functioned at the intellectual level of a six-year-old. Plunkitt's lawyer contended that it was easy for the police to manipulate Murdock, because Bobby wanted the officers to like him and would say whatever the police wanted him to say. The attorney for the state acknowledged that Murdock was mentally retarded but, like a child, he could indeed tell the truth. In addition, the attorney for the state argued that the police did not attempt to coerce Murdock, and only asked him direct questions.

The appeals court in Kentucky overturned Plunkitt's conviction because the court believed that the confession was coerced, and that Bobby Murdock was not competent. The Kentucky Supreme Court, however, reversed the decision of the appeals court and ruled that the confession was not coerced. Moreover the state Supreme Court ruled that the testimony of Bobby Murdock was acceptable, because a mentally retarded person is able to tell the truth. The case was then appealed to the U.S. Supreme Court.

The Supreme Court has accepted this case.

Smelkinson v. University of Oregon

After considerable debate, the State of Arkansas passed a law requiring that Creationism be included as an alternative explanation to evolution in introductory biology courses in Arkansas public high schools, as well as public universities and colleges in Arkansas.

Janice Smelkinson took a biology course at Ozark State University, in Arkansas, as part of her overall undergraduate education. Although Ms. Smelkinson excelled in the course, she did not subscribe to the Creationist material that was included in the course. In fact, she had told her professor "Creationism is not science, and should not be included in a science course." Ms. Smelkinson later decided to major in biology and was regarded as an exceptional student.

In her senior year, Janice Smelkinson did very well on her Graduate Record Exams and applied to graduate programs throughout the United States. One of the places that Smelkinson applied to was the Biology Department at the University of Oregon. Although she was a finalist, the department turned her down for acceptance and financial assistance. The Department Chair, Edwin Goldberger, wrote that Smelkinson was rejected because "your undergraduate biology preparation is weaker when compared to other finalists who concentrated on pure biology, not pseudo-science." Smelkinson was accepted at three other graduate school biology departments and now attends the University of Wisconsin-Madison.

Smelkinson brought suit in federal district court against the University of Oregon for rejecting her in spite of her high Graduate Record scores and outstanding letters of recommendation. She contended that she was turned down for only one reason, the inclusion of Creationism in her Arkansas biology course.

Smelkinson's lawyers argued that the U.S. Constitution guarantees "Full Faith and Credit shall given in each state to the public Acts, Records, and judicial Proceedings of every other State." They contended that the University of Oregon, as an arm of the State of Oregon, was not giving full faith and credit to the public records of Ozark State University, a part of the Arkansas government.

The State of Oregon contended that the "full faith and credit" clause did not mean that one state could impose its political values on another state. The lawyers representing Oregon also contended that curriculum is a matter that is reserved to the states, and that the courts should not get in the business of favoring one state's curriculum over another state's curriculum. Furthermore, Oregon cautioned the courts against either writing or approving curriculum.

Smelkinson won at the district court level. The court ruled that the University of Oregon was being arbitrary when it downgraded the value of an introductory college biology course in Arkansas that contained controversial information.

According to the judge, the course was taught by a qualified instructor, course materials were appropriate and the college was fully accredited. Consequently, the court held that an A in the Arkansas biology course was equivalent to an A in any other state. Furthermore, the district court ordered that the University should admit Smelkinson based on the strength of her total record. The University then appealed to the U.S. Court of Appeals in San Francisco.

The court of appeals overruled the district court on the basis that graduate school admission policies are reserved to the states, and the courts do not have a role in establishing admission policies or procedures.

The matter has been appealed to the U.S. Supreme Court, and the Supreme Court has agreed to hear the case.

Marcus v. North Carolina Roads Commission

The Heritage Vista real estate development firm completed the final stages of Riverview Retirement Community on the Cape Fear River in North Carolina. The Riverview Community is a full service, gated, retirement complex that appeals to upper-income seniors who seek an active and secure retirement in the beautiful North Carolina Coastal Plain. Riverview offers everything from golf courses, tennis courts, hiking trails and indoor activities to nursing care.

Mr. Jan Marcus, a hog farmer, purchased a large parcel of land that was adjacent to the Riverview Retirement Community and expanded his hog farm operation. The Marcus land purchase and expansion was within the law because the land was zoned for agricultural purposes. Nevertheless, the management and the residents of the retirement community became enraged at the possibility of being so close to the hog farm. The Riverview Community was particularly concerned about odors that would come from the Marcus farm, and took their case to the Governor.

Six months later, the North Carolina Roads Commission altered a regional highway plan, including a newly planned road to run through the Marcus Hog Farm. In fact, according to the new plan, a cloverleaf exit was to be placed directly in the middle of the Marcus property and the farm would no longer be able to function for any private use. The Roads Commission employed the power of "eminent domain" and offered Mr. Marcus a fair market price for the property.

Marcus refused to accept the check, and instead brought a suit in the state courts against the Roads Commission on the basis of the Fourteenth Amendment. The attorney for Mr. Marcus noted that the Amendment said that no state can "deprive any person of life, liberty and property, without due process of law." Marcus argued that the plans for the road were changed after the retirement community complained to the Governor, and that the new road plans only served political purposes. Marcus noted that the developers of the retirement community were negligent in not purchasing the vacant property.

At the trial, the State of North Carolina argued that due process had been utilized, and that the whole matter was reserved to the state by the Tenth Amendment. The State of North Carolina said that the road plans were changed to accommodate increasing residential land use in the Coastal Plain. The State cautioned the courts to keep out of the highly technical area of road planning.

The state trial court ruled in favor of Mr. Marcus. The court held that Marcus had obtained the property legally and that the same property had been available to the retirement community. The court contended that the retirement community could have insured that the vacant property would be compatible with their needs by simply buying it. Instead, the court ruled, the retirement community used the political process to correct their mistake, manipulating highway planning and eminent domain to achieve their ends. The trial court held that the rights of Mr. Marcus had been trampled upon, and the State should cease all road construction planning as it related to the Marcus farm.

The State of North Carolina appealed the decision to the U.S. District Court of Appeals, and argued that land use planning and road construction were reserved to the state by the U.S. Constitution. The state contended that its normal processes were used to make the highway construction plans and that Marcus was offered a fair price for the hog farm. The attorneys for Marcus contended that his rights as an American citizen were violated by the State of North Carolina, and that he should be able to pursue his livelihood as a hog farmer.

The U.S. Court of Appeals in Richmond overturned the trial court's decision and ruled that that it is a matter that is reserved to the states, and that Mr. Marcus had been offered fair compensation for the property.

The case has been appealed to the U.S. Supreme Court. The Court has accepted the case.